Stories of JEWISH DAYTON

Stories of
JEWISH
DAYTON

Marshall Weiss

THE
History
PRESS

Published by The History Press
Charleston, SC
www.historypress.com

Copyright © 2021 by Marshall Weiss
All rights reserved

Postcards courtesy of the Dayton Metro Library.

First published 2021

Manufactured in the United States

ISBN 9781467149440

Library of Congress Control Number: 2021937137

Notice: The information in this book is true and complete to the best of our knowledge. It is offered without guarantee on the part of the author or The History Press. The author and The History Press disclaim all liability in connection with the use of this book.

All rights reserved. No part of this book may be reproduced or transmitted in any form whatsoever without prior written permission from the publisher except in the case of brief quotations embodied in critical articles and reviews.

To Joan and Dr. Charlie Knoll, the greatest champions of the Dayton Jewish Observer *over its twenty-five-year history. Your love of the Gem City and passion to right its wrongs are an inspiration.*

CONTENTS

Acknowledgements 9
Introduction 13

1. The Most Important Caterer in U.S. Jewish History 15
2. Dance as an Exchange of Humanity: The Schwarz Sisters 22
3. A 60-Year Friendship 112 Years in the Making 26
4. How the Dailies Covered Jewish Life Before
    Local Jewish Papers Were Here 34
5. Aid for the Transients 43
6. The Spanish Flu of 1918–19: "So Many Hearts are
    Overwhelmed with Sorrow" 50
7. A Historic Zionist Concert at Memorial Hall 62
8. John H. Patterson, NCR, Oakwood and the
    Jewish Community 67
9. How the 1917 Battle of Jerusalem Surrender Flag
    Ended up in Greenville, Ohio 98
10. Jews and Dayton's Booze Trade 107
11. Victory Day: Jews From the Former Soviet Union
    Recall the Nazi Surrender 126
12. Black/Jewish Relations: From the Dayton Riots
    Through School Desegregation 130

Bibliography 155
About the Author 157

ACKNOWLEDGEMENTS

Thanks to the following for their expertise, assistance and wisdom:

- ◊ Cathy Gardner, the CEO of the Jewish Federation of Greater Dayton, for energetically championing Jewish journalism in the Miami Valley and for entrusting me with the Miami Valley Jewish Genealogy and History project.

- ◊ Curt Dalton, visual resources manager at Dayton History, who reviewed this manuscript. A prolific author of books about Dayton history, Curt has generously helped guide me when I've been utterly stumped.

- ◊ Martin Gottlieb, retired *Dayton Daily News* editorial writer, who has served as advisor to the *Dayton Jewish Observer* since 2014 and reviewed this manuscript. Martin's gentle, thoughtful dedication to clarity has helped me sharpen my craft.

- ◊ Mark Bernstein, the author of *Grand Eccentrics—Turning the Century: Dayton and the Inventing of America*, who also reviewed this manuscript. I can't thank him enough for reaching out to me when he moved back to the Dayton area.

Acknowledgements

- Bill Stolz, formerly an archivist with Special Collections and Archives, Wright State University, and now with Dayton Metro Library, who steadfastly aided with every possible request.

- Joe Weber, an associate archivist at the Jacob Rader Marcus Center of the American Jewish Archives, for his speed in tracking down materials and their enthusiasm.

- Joan and Dr. Charlie Knoll for their generous support of this venture and their love of Jewish Dayton.

- John Rodrigue and Ashley Hill at The History Press, for their commitment to the highest editorial standards and for their patience, wisdom and understanding.

- Samuel Dorf, a University of Dayton associate professor of musicology and the first and current chair of the Miami Valley Jewish Genealogy and History Advisory Committee, whose excitement for local history is palpable.

- Gwen Nalls and Daniel L. Baker for taking me down a road I knew so little about.

- Eileen Litchfield of Greenville, who tipped me off about the 1917 Jerusalem surrender flag artifact at the Garst Museum.

- Marcia Burick and Helen Lefkowitz Horowitz for sharing so many anecdotes about their families.

- Meredith Cline for sharing her grandfather Joseph T. Cline's memoirs with me.

- Tina S. Ratcliff, Montgomery County Records and Information manager, and Amy Czubak, archives technician, who located early racially restrictive deeds in Montgomery County.

- Janet Bednarek, a professor and former chair of the history department at the University of Dayton, who helped me better understand the "hows" and "whys" of racial restrictions.

Acknowledgements

- ◊ Edward J. Roach, historian and resources program manager at Dayton Aviation Heritage National Historical Park, for directing me to primary materials about the Wright family's move to Hawthorn Hill instead of Dayton View.

- ◊ Christian Gray of Oakwood, currently a law student at the Georgetown University Law Center, for pointing out an article in the *Dayton Daily News* that reported on the first major Klan event in the Dayton area.

- ◊ Sunny Jane Morton, editor of *Ohio Genealogy News*, who invited me to write an article for the Summer 2020 issue and also gave me permission to distribute the piece. I've published it in the *Observer*, and here, you'll find an expanded version as chapter 4.

- ◊ Longtime Dayton trial lawyer David C. Greer, who has written extensively about the history of Dayton's legal community, for suggesting I look at the Meyer Ostrov case.

- ◊ My family—Donna, Levi and Adina Weiss—for listening to all the stories.

INTRODUCTION

This book is a thank-you to the Jewish community of my adoptive home, Dayton, Ohio. It honors twenty-five years of Jewish journalism here in the form of the *Dayton Jewish Observer*, which the Jewish Federation has entrusted to my care since I was hired to create a Jewish newspaper for the Miami Valley in January 1996. It's been quite a ride.

In short order, I fell in love with Dayton, its Jewish community, the history of both and how they intertwine. Dayton has been very good to me and my family.

Stories of Jewish Dayton grew out of my first book, *Jewish Community of Dayton* (Arcadia, 2018), a visual history of Jewish life in the city that emphasized what set Jewish Dayton apart: Arthur Welsh, the first-known Jewish airplane pilot in America; the first National Workshop on Catholic-Jewish Relations, held here in 1971; opera star Jan Peerce giving the final performance of his career with the acclaimed Beth Abraham Youth Chorale in 1982.

For that project, I composed a list of all the tall tales I had heard about Jewish Dayton to find out which were true, which were false and which were somewhere in between. This was how I stumbled onto long-forgotten episodes that kept pulling me back to find out more. After *Jewish Community of Dayton* came out, the Jewish Federation offered me the opportunity to manage the Dayton Jewish Genealogical Society as a project of the federation. I proposed to Jewish Federation CEO Cathy Gardner and to the Jewish Genealogy Society's then-president Molly Blumer that, along

Introduction

with running the society's operations, we could expand it to encompass the historical research and writing I love so much. That was the beginning of Miami Valley Jewish Genealogy and History and our well-followed Facebook page, "Growing up Jewish in Miami Valley, Ohio."

To continue with this work is a joy. Eight of the twelve chapters in this book came out of the research I've pursued since 2018. All of the chapters have been published in some form in the pages of the *Observer*. Here, they've been updated and expanded.

Several people weave their way in and out of multiple chapters of this book. One who is present almost throughout is Rabbi David Lefkowitz, the greatest leader of Dayton's Jewish community of his time and one of the greatest leaders in Dayton's general community in those days. Throughout his twenty years in Dayton, Rabbi Lefkowitz had his hand in virtually every cause to improve the quality of life for all in the Gem City. In these pages, he almost takes on the role of a familiar guide.

As you read *Stories of Jewish Dayton*, you'll notice that two chapters in particular comprise half the length of the book. Both are about racial hatred and race relations: the first is from the beginning of the twentieth century, and the second is from the century's end. Much of this history has been forgotten or misunderstood—or possibly never learned at all. Now, as communities across the United States attempt to reckon with and dismantle racism once again, maybe this time, we can learn from what went wrong in the past.

In several ways, the challenges our Jewish community faces today are not so different from those we stared down a century ago. Even in the face of fearful setbacks, I believe the American dream lives. For those in America who haven't yet fully tasted the American dream, it is our responsibility to help that happen to the best of our ability, as Jews and as Americans.

1
THE MOST IMPORTANT CATERER IN U.S. JEWISH HISTORY

It's no exaggeration to say that the person who set in motion the divisions in American Judaism we know today is buried at Temple Israel's Riverview Cemetery.

In 1883, when Prussian-born Jew Gustave "Gus" Lindeman was a celebrated caterer in Cincinnati, Rabbi Isaac Mayer Wise hired him to prepare the banquet to celebrate Hebrew Union College's first rabbinic ordination ceremony and the Union of American Hebrew Congregations' tenth anniversary. Wise had founded both institutions. Wise, the architect of Reform Judaism in America, hoped to unite American synagogues and rabbis within a broad coalition that would bring traditionalists and reformers together. More than one hundred rabbis and layleaders from seventy-six Jewish congregations around the country showed up in Cincinnati for the July 11, 1883 ordination ceremony at Wise's Plum Street Temple.

At the banquet, which was held afterward at the Highland House on Mt. Adams, Lindeman served a *treyf* (unkosher) menu, albeit without pork. No one knows for certain whether it was Wise or his committee who approved the menu, or if Lindeman acted on his own, though it's unlikely Wise would have intentionally provoked his guests when his aim was to bring them together.

Cincinnati's Reform German Jews did tend to eat treyf, except for pork. But because of the "Treyfa Banquet," outraged traditionalists would go on to establish Orthodox and then Conservative Judaism as formal religious movements in America.

A Popular Caterer

Lindeman was born in 1845 in Prussia. He first showed up in Cincinnati's city directory in 1867 as a barkeeper in a saloon. By the 1870s, Cincinnati newspapers described him as a fashionable, popular caterer.

When Cincinnati's German Jewish Allemania Club opened its new building at Fourth Street and Central Avenue on May 1, 1879, Lindeman catered the event. The *Cincinnati Enquirer* described the opening as "one of the most brilliant social events of the season" and "one of the most enjoyable affairs that has ever been celebrated in this city." Among the 350 guests was Ohio governor Richard Moore Bishop. Over the music of an orchestra, Lindeman's dinner for the "Hebrew society" included oysters, various meats and vanilla ice cream—all violations of kashrut—but no pork.

After the Treyfa Banquet, when the more traditional delegates returned to their homes, they spread the word about the debacle through Jewish and even general newspapers. One account in a Jewish newspaper was written by Henrietta Szold, who was there from Baltimore with her father, Rabbi Benjamin Szold; she would later found Hadassah, the

Left: By the 1870s, Prussian-born Jew Gustave "Gus" Lindeman was one of Cincinnati's most popular caterers. *Courtesy of Ellen Notbohm.*

Right: Rabbi Isaac Mayer Wise of Cincinnati, the architect of Reform Judaism in the United States. *Courtesy of the Jacob Rader Marcus Center of the American Jewish Archives.*

The menu for the "Treyfa Banquet," July 11, 1883. *Courtesy of the Jacob Rader Marcus Center of the American Jewish Archives.*

women's Zionist organization. In Wise's English-language publication, the *American Israelite*, he blamed the error on Lindeman. However, in his German-language publication, *Die Deborah*, he wrote that his committee had ordered the meal.

The menu for the Treyfa Banquet, held to honor delegates of the Union of American Hebrew Congregations, shows that no pork was served—although diners could eat clams, crab, frog and shrimp, among other non-kosher items.

In a 2018 essay for Jewish Telegraphic Agency, Brandeis University professor of American Jewish history Jonathan Sarna wrote that Wise knew the banquet was a blunder. Sarna highly doubted that Wise was to blame. "After all, he himself kept a kosher home—his second wife, the daughter of an Orthodox rabbi, insisted upon it," Sarna explained. "But he was not the kind of leader who believed in making apologies. Instead, he lashed out against his critics, insisting that the dietary laws had lost all validity, and ridiculed them for advocating 'kitchen Judaism.'"

Line in the Sand

In 1885, the Reform movement would codify its eschewal of Jewish dietary laws in article 4 of the Central Conference of American Rabbis' (CCAR) Declaration of Principles, known today as the Pittsburgh Platform:

> *We hold that all such Mosaic and rabbinical laws as regulate diet, priestly purity, and dress originated in ages and under the influence of ideas entirely foreign to our present mental and spiritual state. They fail to impress the modern Jew with a spirit of priestly holiness; their observance in our days is apt rather to obstruct than to further modern spiritual elevation.*

Wise, who also founded the CCAR, presided over the meeting. His line in the sand led American Judaism to splinter into two and, later, three movements. Traditionalists established the Jewish Theological Seminary (JTS) in New York in 1886; two years later, they established the Union of Orthodox Jewish Congregations of America. JTS and the Orthodox Union eventually parted ways in the years after Rabbi Solomon Schechter arrived from England to lead JTS in 1902. JTS would become the flagship institution of the Conservative Jewish movement.

Making a Name in Dayton

In 1895, Lindeman moved to Dayton, where he lived until his death in 1927. He made a name for himself as the steward of the Dayton City Club, a non-Jewish social club at the southwest corner of First and Main Streets. A 1902 advertisement in the *Dayton Daily News* for Rising Sun Baking Powder is centered around a testimonial from Lindeman in his role as the Dayton City Club's steward.

Lindeman departed the Dayton City Club in 1908 to strike out on his own, opening Lindeman's Restaurant and Catering Business in a storefront at the Victoria Theater. He was also a trustee of the International Stewards' Association and a founder and president of Dayton's chapter. Among his catering clients was A.M. Kittredge, the president of the Barney & Smith Car Company.

The Great Flood of 1913 and its damage to the Victoria Theater marked the end of Lindeman's restaurant. He managed at least one more restaurant,

Above: Gus Lindeman served as the celebrated steward of the Dayton City Club from 1895 until about 1909. *Courtesy of the Dayton Metro Library.*

Left: Gus Lindeman in his later years with his wife, Henrietta. *From the collection of Mark Dues.*

Lindeman's granddaughters, sisters Hermene (*left*) and Josephine Schwarz (*right*), the founders of the Dayton Ballet. *Courtesy of the* Dayton Daily News *Collection, Special Collections and Archives, Wright State University.*

Maharg's Blue Room; served as a manager and steward of the Dayton Country Club from 1913 to 1917; and continued his catering business from his home, 49 West Holt Street, until 1925. But his contributions to Dayton and its Jewish history don't end there.

Lindeman's granddaughters, sisters Josephine and Hermene Schwarz, founded the Schwarz School of Dance in 1927 and the Experimental Group for Young Dancers in 1937—later renamed the Dayton Ballet—the second-oldest ballet company in the United States.

Would American Judaism have ended up splintering had there been no Treyfa Banquet? Most likely. But Lindeman's most famous meal is what set it in motion.

2

DANCE AS AN EXCHANGE OF HUMANITY

The Schwarz Sisters

"I wanted to do whatever my sister did," Carol Ann Shockley recalls. "She was three and a half years older than me. And I wanted to be just like her. She wanted to dance." Carol Ann's sister was the late Jeraldyne Blunden, the founder of Jeraldyne's School of the Dance and Dayton Contemporary Dance Company (DCDC), which celebrated its fiftieth anniversary in 2018. Blunden was the recipient of a MacArthur Foundation "Genius" Award five years before her death in 1999.

Two decades before DCDC's founding, in 1948, Jeraldyne and Carol Ann's mother and their friends' mothers were looking for a dance studio for their girls. "Back in those days, it was hard," Carol Ann says. "The only dance studios were White. And everybody [the studios] said the typical: 'There's no room, our classes are closed.'"

The mothers went to see Dayton Ballet founders Josephine and Hermene Schwarz, who had run their own dance studio for two decades. "Miss Jo [Josephine Schwarz] told them, 'We'd love to teach your children. But I'm sorry to say they can't come to our school. If they do, we'll lose business. We can't afford to lose business. You find the place, and we'll come there.'" The manager of the Linden Recreation Center at 334 Norwood Avenue on the West Side let the mothers hold dance classes there on Saturdays.

As soon as eight-year-old Jeraldyne would walk home from dance class, she'd teach Carol Ann everything she had learned that week from Miss Jo. Debbie Blunden-Diggs, Jeraldyne's daughter, can see the defunct Linden Recreation Center from her studio at 840 Germantown Street. Debbie is

Josephine (*left*) and Hermene Schwarz (*right*). *Courtesy of the* Dayton Daily News *Collection, Special Collections and Archives, Wright State University.*

Josephine Schwarz (*back, fourth from the left*) at the Linden Center Dance School with Jeraldyne Blunden (*back right*) and her sister Carol Ann Shockley (*front, fourth from the left*). *Courtesy of DCDC.*

Carol Ann Shockley (*left*), Jeraldyne Blunden's sister, with Blunden's daughter, DCDC artistic director Debbie Blunden-Diggs. *Courtesy of Marshall Weiss.*

the artistic director of DCDC and the director of Jeraldyne's School of the Dance.

The Schwarz sisters, staunch supporters of Jeraldyne's dance career, saw to it that their star pupil attended the American Dance Festival in Connecticut. There, Jeraldyne learned from Martha Graham, José Limon, George Balanchine and James Truitte.

When Miss Jo asked nineteen-year-old Jeraldyne to take over the Linden Center Dance School, Jeraldyne's School of the Dance was born. "Jeraldyne was training dancers to go out on auditions with companies," Carol Ann, who worked for her sister, remembers. They were landing at Dance Theatre of Harlem, the American Dance Festival and the Alvin Ailey American Dance Theatre. "And Jeraldyne said to me one Saturday, 'Carol Ann, why am I training these dancers and sending them away? Why don't I start my own group?' I said, 'Why don't you?' The rest is history. And she was just fabulous at it."

The Schwarzes, Carol Ann said, stood behind Jeraldyne and DCDC—a company rooted in the African American experience—200 percent. "Miss Jo would judge auditions for the company," she says. "And when Jeraldyne had concerns or problems or issues, she would call Miss Jo and ask for advice." Debbie remembers how the Schwarz sisters mentored her mother and stayed very close to her through it all as the company rose from regional to national and then international acclaim. "Miss Jo and Miss Hermene, in my memory, were always at the performances," Debbie said. "They were always a significant influence and part of the thought process of how Jeraldyne built this company. I remember when the company auditioned for membership into what used to be called the Northeast Regional Ballet Association. It was under the eyes and watch of Miss Jo, because they [Dayton Ballet] were one of the founding companies in that association."

Debbie herself began dancing at the age of five in 1965 with the Schwarz School of Dance, which, by then, was integrated. Miss Hermene was her first teacher. After seven years with the Schwarz School, Debbie joined DCDC at the age of twelve; by seventeen, she had garnered national recognition for her choreography. She recalls the Schwarzes as regal in posture and personality. "They were very strict and demanding but very caring in all the same breath," Debbie said. "They were huge advocates of the artform and what it gave you outside of just being a dancer." This, Debbie said, included discipline, focus, the ability to be strategic and problem-solving skills. Debbie described her mother as an incredible nurturer and "a huge disciplinarian." The Schwarz sisters and her mother, Debbie added, had a desire to make the world a better place, with dance as a form of diplomacy, an exchange of humanity. "And it [was] really started by a group of mothers just wanting something quality, something better for their children. That is, I believe, the plight of all parents. You just want something better for your child than what people are just willing to give you."

DCDC founder Jeraldyne Blunden. *Courtesy of DCDC.*

3

A 60-YEAR FRIENDSHIP 112 YEARS IN THE MAKING

The summer of 2018 marked the sixtieth anniversary of the opening of Goldman Union Camp Institute, an overnight summer camp of the Reform Jewish movement, in Zionsville, Indiana. It also marked the sixtieth anniversary of a dear friendship that began there between Marcia Burick and Helen Lefkowitz Horowitz. As they discovered in that 1958 summer, they were rekindling a family friendship that began in 1906, when their grandfathers—both rabbis in Dayton—first met.

Helen's grandfather was Rabbi David Lefkowitz of Dayton's Reform congregation, B'nai Yeshurun—now Temple Israel—from 1900 to 1920. Marcia's grandfather Rabbi Samuel Burick served the Lithuanian Orthodox-Jewish congregation, Beth Abraham Synagogue, from 1906 to 1949. The rabbis, who came from distinctly different Jewish backgrounds, developed a close bond. Together, they worked for the betterment of the Jewish community and to bring it closer together.

Today, Marcia lives in Northampton, Massachusetts; Helen lives much of the year in Cambridge, Massachusetts, and the rest of the year in Pasadena, California.

David Lefkowitz was born in Eperies, Hungary, in 1875. His widowed mother brought him and his two brothers to the United States around 1881. Unable to support the family, she abandoned Lefkowitz and one of his brothers at the Hebrew Orphan Asylum in New York. Lefkowitz lived there from 1883 to 1889. "It was a German Jewish philanthropy to civilize Russian-Jewish children," Helen said of the orphanage. "While he went to

Left: Helen Lefkowitz Horowitz, the granddaughter of Sadie and Rabbi David Lefkowitz. *Courtesy of Helen Lefkowitz Horowitz.*

Right: Marcia Burick, the granddaughter of Lillian and Rabbi Samuel Burick. *Courtesy of Marcia Burick.*

City University, he did work at the Hebrew orphanage as a proctor to the children," she added. "And then, it was not an unusual thing that there was a connection to Hebrew Union College in Cincinnati."

Lefkowitz arrived in Dayton in 1900, beginning his work at B'nai Yeshurun as a student rabbi. "My grandfather, in the year 1900, was in his final year at Hebrew Union College [HUC] in Cincinnati," Helen said. He met his wife, Sadie Braham, when he boarded in her parents' home. Helen said HUC's founder, Rabbi Isaac Mayer Wise, gave her grandfather a wooden Havdalah spice box before Wise died in March 1900; the spice box was passed on to her.

In Dayton, Lefkowitz quickly gained a reputation as a social reformer and sought-after speaker in the general community. Non-Jews began attending the young rabbi's sermons at his temple, located on Jefferson Street, between First and Second Streets. He began receiving invitations to speak at civic events. Lefkowitz would also attempt to bridge gaps among the distinct groups that comprised Dayton's Jewish community.

"My grandfather," Marcia said of Samuel Burick, "had come from Poland where he was trained, and then he went to Canada and then to Gary,

Left: Rabbi David Lefkowitz served B'nai Yeshurun from 1900 to 1920. *Courtesy of Dayton History.*

Right: Rabbi Samuel Burick, shown here at the age of thirty in 1911, served at Beth Abraham Synagogue from 1906 to 1949. *From the collection of Marcia Burick.*

B'nai Yeshurun's building from 1892 to 1927, which was located on the east side of Jefferson Street, between First and Second Streets. *Courtesy of Temple Israel.*

Indiana. There was another wife who died but nobody ever talks about. And then he came to Dayton, single, maybe six years after Rabbi Lefkowitz came. Rabbi Lefkowitz greeted and welcomed my grandfather into the community and invited him to the temple. And they became friends."

But the leaders of Burick's Orthodox synagogue were not pleased with this. "The powers that be at the synagogue, the Wayne Avenue Synagogue," Marcia said, "wrote him [Burick] a letter, castigating him for going to be with a Reform rabbi. I'm not sure castigating is the right term."

Helen picked up the story. "I think they censured him," she said of Rabbi Burick, who was about twenty-five years old then. "My grandfather always laughed about it in later days," Marcia continued. "He said that he got the *hechsher* [kosher certification] in reverse. He said, instead of the Orthodox rabbi giving the hechsher to the Reform rabbi, Rabbi Lefkowitz gave him the hechsher of approval."

Members of Dayton's Weisman family brought a cousin, Lillian Solnetzky, over from Russia in 1908 to become Burick's bride. "How could they stand to have a single rabbi?" Marcia said of her grandfather's congregants.

Out of Zionsville

Marcia and Helen met through NFTY, the National Federation of Temple Youth. "I was secretary of Ohio Valley Federation of Temple Youth," Marcia says, "and I spent a lot of time my senior year going with Elmer and Dorothy Moyer. Dorothy and my mother [Rae Burick] did every philanthropic thing there was to do in Dayton together."

The Reform movement had put Elmer Moyer in charge of selecting the site for a regional Reform overnight summer camp. "I traveled with them on four or five different weekends, all over the area," Marcia continued. "And they found a camp in Zionsville, Indiana. Within two or three months, they bought the camp and got it ready for the summer of '58, which was the summer I had graduated from high school [Fairview] and was about to go off to college." The camp hired Marcia for that first summer as its secretary, "a fancy term for the person who stocked the canteen and carried the laundry into town, and fell in love with the president of NFTY," she quipped.

Helen, whose father was a rabbi in Shreveport, Louisiana, was president of the Southern Federation of Temple Youth. She arrived at the new camp as a high schooler. "We got to chatting, because Marcia sat sort of in the front as you walked into the building," Helen said. "She was older and gorgeous, of course. I learned that she was about to go to Wellesley College. Wellesley was on my radar list. So, Marcia was there when I arrived as a first-year student, and she was living in a dormitory across the way."

When Helen first arrived at Wellesley, she said, "the first thing Marcia did was to call me to say, 'I've got tickets to the World Series, and I've got one for you, Helen.' I said, 'I'm terribly sorry, Marcia. But I'm not interested in baseball.'" Helen didn't realize how important sports were to the Burick family. Marcia's father, Si, was the longtime sports editor of the *Dayton Daily News*. "Well, she managed to forgive me over time!" Helen said.

Marcia would go on to work in government at various times in her life. "I taught a course on reinventing government and government reform in a number of places," she said, including in Lithuania and the Baltics, where she's searched for her roots.

Helen received her master's and PhD in American civilization from Harvard, and she became a history professor with a specialty in American cultural history. She's taught at MIT, Union College, Scripps College, the University of Southern California and on the faculty of Smith College from 1988 until her retirement in 2010. During her twenty-two years at Smith, Helen lived only a few miles from Marcia. "Marcia and I used to always go out and have a glass of wine at the Hotel Northampton on her birthday," Helen said.

One Passover Seder that Marcia hosted ended up being a who's who of descendants of Dayton rabbis, including Helen; a great-granddaughter of Rabbi Philip Weisman, who served Beth Jacob in the 1890s; and a granddaughter of Rabbi Selwyn Ruslander, Temple Israel's rabbi from 1947 until his death in 1969.

The German/Eastern European Jewish Divide

In the early 1900s, the established, acculturated German Jews—successful merchants and professionals who had arrived in Dayton beginning in the 1840s—comprised the Reform Jewish community. They lived downtown in the area of North Robert Boulevard.

Their poorer Eastern European cousins, who had started to arrive in the 1880s because of raging antisemitism in the Russian Empire, made their homes in the vicinity of Wayne Avenue, between Fifth and Wyoming Streets in the East End, down to South Park. Dayton's Eastern European Jews prayed at Orthodox synagogues: Russian Jews at Beth Jacob, 358 East Wyoming Street; and Lithuanian Jews at Beth Abraham, 530 South Wayne Avenue.

Helen said the grandfathers refused to let the German/Eastern European Jewish divide stand in their way. "They worked at it, even though it was initially criticized," she said.

Crisis and need ultimately nudged segments of Dayton's Jewish community closer, albeit reluctantly. In 1910, Lefkowitz brought together businessmen from his German Jewish congregation to establish the Federation of Jewish Charities of Dayton to provide impoverished Jews—generally the Eastern Europeans—with interest-free loans, food, clothing and coal.

Two years later, the Jewish Federation formally asked officers of Beth Abraham and Beth Jacob synagogues to send representatives to serve on its board. The federation's minutes from the time indicate that Beth Abraham did, but Beth Jacob did not respond; the congregation's sense of dignity may have been the reason.

In 1927, Harold Silver, of the Bureau of Jewish Social Research, wrote that the Jewish immigrants of Eastern Europe "made no secret of the fact that in addition to desiring a kosher ritual and to help the poor in their own spirit, they wanted to show the German Jews that they were not *schnorrers* [moochers] or parasites."

Of the German Jews, Morris D. Waldman, the founder and head of numerous national Jewish programs, wrote in 1916, "It has been customary for the early settler to regard the later arrival as inferior. The tendency on the part of earlier German Jewish settlers to look askance at the later Russian Jewish immigrants was not to be wondered at."

The Great Flood of 1913 and then World War I united Dayton's Jewish community more than ever before. "They worked together on flood relief," Marcia said. "That was the big thing my grandfather talked about. After the flood, when Rabbi Lefkowitz helped rescue people, and then founded the [Dayton] Red Cross [in 1917], he involved my grandfather and grandmother in that." The Jewish Federation, under Lefkowitz's guidance, provided relief loans for those hit hardest by the flood. By 1915, several borrowers could not repay them, and the federation set aside loans "on which payment would be a hardship."

Nine Torah scrolls belonging to Beth Abraham Synagogue were destroyed in the 1913 flood; they were buried at Beth Abraham Cemetery on May

One of the two stone markers where Beth Abraham Synagogue buried nine Torahs that were destroyed in the 1913 flood. The markers were rediscovered at Beth Abraham Cemetery in April 2019. *Courtesy of Marshall Weiss.*

18, 1913, after the Jewish community's procession from Wayne Avenue. Lefkowitz and Beth Jacob Synagogue's rabbi, Mendel Finkelstein, offered words at the Torah burial service along with Burick. When Beth Abraham dedicated a new Torah scroll, which had been brought over from the Russian Empire in September 1913 to begin replacing the nine scrolls destroyed in the flood, Lefkowitz joined Burick to help officiate at the ceremony.

Beth Abraham's wood-frame building had also been washed away in the flood. And when Beth Abraham dedicated its new brick building at the same site in 1918, along with Burick and out-of-town rabbis who addressed the congregation in Yiddish, Lefkowitz delivered a speech in English.

With the increase in transients coming through Dayton, Burick and Lefkowitz worked with the federation to care for those who were Jewish. "He never knew how many people would be at the dinner table," Marcia said of her grandfather.

Beginning in 1916, all segments of Dayton's Jewish community would meet together to raise funds for Jewish war relief in Europe, to increase the number of local Jews enlisting in the armed forces when the United States entered the war and to celebrate the British Balfour Declaration, "in regard to the resettlement of Jerusalem for the Jews after the war."

In 1920, Lefkowitz moved his family to Dallas, where he would serve as rabbi of Temple Emanu-El until his retirement in 1948; he died in 1955. "He is remembered in Dallas mainly for his public opposition to the rise of the KKK," Helen said. "He was outspoken on that at a time when it was considered quite dangerous, particularly for a Jew." Lefkowitz would become the president of the Central Conference of American Rabbis, and later in life, he hosted a radio show in Dallas.

Beth Abraham Synagogue dedicated its new building on South Wayne Avenue, opposite Jones Street, in 1918. *Courtesy of Beth Abraham.*

Burick continued to play a key role aiding observant Jewish transients in consultation with the Jewish Federation. "My grandfather had a stroke, I think in 1948," Marcia said, "and he died in 1957. He was in a wheelchair for all that time, but his mind was there. He could talk softly."

The year after Rabbi Burick's death, Marcia came home from her summer at the Zionsville camp. She told her grandmother, "Bubbie Burick," that she had met Helen Lefkowitz, the granddaughter of Rabbi Lefkowitz. Marcia remembers her grandmother's reaction: "Oh, he was such a mensch. He was such a good friend. Yes, he was so good to us and so welcoming."

4

HOW THE DAILIES COVERED JEWISH LIFE BEFORE LOCAL JEWISH PAPERS WERE HERE

On the afternoon of Wednesday, October 7, 1863, Dayton's forty-plus Jewish families held a grand celebration: the dedication of the first synagogue building in this city of approximately twenty thousand people. Holy Congregation B'nai Yeshurun, now known as Temple Israel, had purchased the building at the northeast corner of Fourth and Jefferson Streets from a Baptist church.

Two local daily newspapers, the *Dayton Journal* (Republican) and the *Daily Empire* (Democratic) presented vivid accounts of the proceedings in their issues the next day. Because of the *Journal*, we know the procession to the new synagogue included "a large number of pretty little girls, dressed in white, beautifully decorated, and they were marching in couples, then young ladies charmingly costumed, and exquisitely decked with head dresses and scarfs, succeeded them." We also know from the *Journal* that "prominent members" of the congregation followed them, carrying three Torah scrolls, "covered with the richest velvet cloth, with crowns in decoration, followed under a canopy."

"The Jews may well be proud of their beautiful place of worship," the *Daily Empire* announced to its readers.

Over the next few days, each newspaper ran corrections about the event. Both had listed the name of the congregation's new rabbi, "Rev. Mr. Delbanco," incorrectly. It's possible that the congregation printed his name incorrectly in the event program, and the papers likely followed suit. Not only did the *Daily Empire* run this correction, it also reprinted the

Dayton Daily Empire.

THE DAYTON EVENING HERALD.

THE DAYTON DAILY NEWS.

DAYTON JOURNAL

Local newspapers gave a fair shake to Dayton's Jewish community. *Courtesy of the Dayton Metro Library.*

entire article with two items that were not mentioned in the first version: a notation that "the eldest members of the congregation" carried the Torah scrolls in the procession to the new synagogue building and that the mayor and city council were in attendance. This revised version of the article begins with a clear explanation: "By request of our Jewish friends, we republish the account of the dedication of the Synagogue…for the purpose of correcting errors which were made in the original." More than 150 years later, I am glad the *Daily Empire* did this not only because it clarified the record, but also because it added even more detail to help later generations better visualize the scene.

It's one of the numerous examples in Dayton's daily newspapers—and across party lines—of their interest in and detailed coverage of this small Jewish community from its near-beginnings through the twentieth century. This was long before a Jewish press raised its own voice in Dayton, though the Jews here could look for some coverage of our community in Cincinnati's *American Israelite* (established 1854) and the *Ohio Jewish Chronicle*, based in Columbus (established 1922).

The first known Jewish newspaper in Dayton, the *Dayton Jewish Life*, ran for about a year (from the end of 1917 to the end of 1918). Temple Israel published the *Dayton Jewish Record* between 1934 and 1935. It wasn't until 1958 that Dayton had its own Jewish newspaper again—the *Dayton Jewish Chronicle*—this time, until 1995. Since 1996, I've had the honor of serving as the editor of the Gem City's current Jewish newspaper, the *Dayton Jewish Observer*.

When I began my research into Dayton's Jewish history, I was pleasantly surprised to find that the local dailies were such treasured resources. I read for myself that the earliest Jews to arrive in Dayton became active participants in the betterment of the general community and that they were given a seat at the table—and in situations where they weren't, the daily papers would call it out.

Early Jewish Life in Dayton

The first Jews to settle in Dayton came in the 1840s. They emigrated from Prussia and Bavaria, where they were prohibited from certain professions, places they could live and, often, from legally marrying. They generally met with success in Dayton, working their way up from peddlers to shop owners.

When the first key leader of Dayton's Jewish community, Joseph Lebensburger, died at the age of sixty-five in 1877, the *Dayton Journal* reported: "He was largely known in the vicinity and highly esteemed." We also learn from the *Journal* that he was a Mason, an Odd Fellow, a member of the Ancient Order of United Workmen and a member of the Red Men.

As far back as 1860, the *Daily Empire* sporadically included information about upcoming Jewish holidays, their significance and how they were observed. In 1865, the publication included an account of a local Jewish wedding. "We had the pleasure of witnessing on yesterday afternoon the lengthy and peculiarly impressive ceremonies of a Jewish marriage at the house of Mr. L. Jacobs," the *Empire* reported on August 15, 1865. "May success attend the new married pair in the realization of their fondest hopes in the married life." The *Journal* also offered information about Jewish holidays and included goings-on of members of the Jewish community on its society page. "'A HAPPY NEW YEAR!' That is the Manner in which Jew Greets Jew To-Day," read a *Daily Herald* headline on September 14, 1882.

That year, the *Daily Herald* also included in its society column an item about an employee with Dayton's German Jewish social club: "Mr. Joseph Beatus, who so acceptably filled the position of janitor for the Standard Jewish Club during the past nine years has resigned the position greatly to the regret of many members of the club. Joe has gone back to his old business as an optician."

An Affinity for Social Reform

When James M. Cox started the *Dayton Daily News* in 1898, his Democratic newspaper also published information about Jewish holidays and included Jews in its society column. Two years later, with the arrival of Rabbi David Lefkowitz to serve B'nai Yeshurun synagogue, Cox was present at the young Lefkowitz's first sermon in Dayton. In short order, Lefkowitz became known for his sermons on social reform.

Cox—a progressive Democrat who would later serve two terms in the U.S. House of Representatives, three terms as Ohio's governor and would be the 1920 Democratic presidential nominee—saw to it that the *Dayton Daily News* began to cover Lefkowitz's lectures. He first showed up in the March 31, 1900 issue of the *Dayton Daily News*, when Cox published the "touching" eulogy Lefkowitz delivered the night before at the synagogue in memory of Rabbi Isaac Mayer Wise, the Cincinnati-based leader of Reform Judaism in America who was also Lefkowitz's teacher.

Dayton Daily News founder and publisher James M. Cox. *Courtesy of the Library of Congress.*

A month later, Lefkowitz appeared in an extensive society item in Cox's paper. The rabbi had officiated at the wedding of Corrine Pollack, daughter of Dayton's successful whiskey wholesaler Isaac Pollack, to a young man from Lexington, Kentucky. As was common in society items of the day, the report described the gowns worn by the women of the wedding party and shared the dinner menu, which shows how Dayton's Reform Jews dined (decidedly not kosher, but still, no pork) in those days. "The banquet hall was beautifully decorated with lilies, palms, white roses and carnations, and the glow of rose-shaded candelabra gave a bewitching radiance to the festive scene," the reader learns of the reception and ball at the Standard Club. "The color scheme of white and green prevailed throughout the house, and the appointments were elegant."

The *Dayton Daily News* also started listing Lefkowitz's upcoming synagogue sermons. Non-Jews began attending Friday night Sabbath services at B'nai Yeshurun to hear what he had to say. And Lefkowitz would receive invitations to deliver lectures to civic groups and for high-profile public occasions, which Cox would also cover. Lefkowitz, described in the *Dayton Daily* as "the thrilling and eloquent leader of the modern Jewish church in this city," delivered the oration at the annual memorial service of Encampment No. 83 Union Veteran Legion in 1902; he gave a speech to the student body of Steele High School; he gave a "stereopticon talk" at Christ Church about the Great Men of Israel in 1903; and he gave the eulogy for the annual memorial services of Gem City Council, No. 3, United Commercial Travelers (traveling salesmen) in 1904.

The *Journal* and *Herald* began listing the rabbi's upcoming sermon topics during that decade, too. They, along with the *Dayton Daily*, also reported on happenings in Dayton's more recently-established synagogues of poorer Orthodox Jewish immigrants who were flooding into America from Eastern Europe—the House of Jacob and the House of Abraham in Dayton's East End—and the multitude of Jewish clubs and service organizations that sprang up in the city at the turn of the twentieth century.

Jewish News Without a Jewish Newspaper

A comfort level became apparent between the local dailies and the somewhat Balkanized segments of Dayton's Jewish community that allowed for open, honest coverage of the Jewish community—in the absence of a sustainable local Jewish newspaper. For Jews who could read English, the daily papers helped them learn about aspects of Jewish life and sensibilities from other parts of the Jewish community that they may not have encountered in their daily lives. This may have nudged segments of the Jewish community closer together in the lead up to the great unifiers that were soon to come: the Great Dayton Flood of 1913 and World War I.

Zionism, which was not yet a settled issue across Judaism's movements, was actively covered, discussed and debated in the dailies, with local Jews weighing in. At the request of the *Dayton Daily*, attorney Ishur L. Jacobson wrote the article "Will the Jew Return to Palestine? How the World War will Affect Zionist Movement," on September 5, 1915.

Rabbi M. Lichtenstein of the Wayne Avenue Synagogue (Beth Abraham) took Rabbi Samuel Mayerberg of the Jefferson Street Temple (B'nai Yeshurun) to task in the March 20, 1921 *Dayton Daily News*, castigating Mayerberg in detail for his statement that the Jews are not a nation but "a race with a religious ideal."

The local Dayton papers widely covered the antisemitic pogroms of Eastern Europe before, during and after World War I. This coverage rallied leaders in Dayton's general community. They gathered publicly with Dayton's Jews, condemned the violent hatred and helped raise funds for its victims. This was documented in detail in those papers.

In 1908, the *Dayton Daily News* published an unsigned editorial below the heading "Unjust Discrimination" in support of the Russian Jews who had immigrated to the United States.

> *In Russia, the believers in the Jewish doctrines are discriminated against to such an extent that they are, today, the poorest, most miserable people on earth. They are denied the privilege of owning the land. Their homes and their property are confiscated. Their women and children are insulted and murdered. Their young men are forced into the army against their wishes and reviled after being forced in. No Jew may hold a commission in the army, so there is no hope for the Jewish young man who is driven into the ranks....A child of a believer in the Jewish faith, brought up in the city of Dayton, is going to be an American citizen.*

On at least one occasion, a political fight within a synagogue spilled over to a daily, with both parties knowingly airing their beefs in the public eye. "Expect Big Doings at Annual Election of House of Jacob" announced a *Dayton Herald* headline on August 2, 1910; the article described a "hot contest" for synagogue president between supporters of longtime president Nathan Bader and Harry Office. "Friends of Office have their 'knives out' for Bader's scalp, and it was said Tuesday that even if Bader does get enough votes to be elected, steps will be taken to prevent him from serving," the *Herald* exclaimed.

After the election, the *Herald* reported on August 8 that by a margin of one vote, "irregularities were alleged in the annual election" and that "court proceedings were threatened to prevent Nathan Bader from again taking his seat as president of the congregation." But on August 15, the *Herald* reported that the conflict was resolved "in the interest of harmony." Bader withdrew from the presidency, although he claimed he was "regularly and legally elected president."

Fair Shake During a Dark Era

The 1920s and 1930s marked the shift to the most antisemitic period among mainstream Americans. A century ago, Dayton's dailies stood firm to give the region's Jews a fair shake.

When Dayton became a hotbed of Ku Klux Klan activity in the early 1920s, the dailies covered it thoroughly. The *Dayton Daily News* trumpeted that it had brought to the attention of the Montgomery County Commission that the county had allowed the Klan to book a meeting for May 26, 1922, which was to be held at the county's war memorial auditorium, Memorial Hall. When the county commission failed to take action to stop the Klan meeting, the *Dayton Daily* reported this and that B'nai Yeshurun's rabbi Samuel Mayerberg, civic and business leader M.J. Gibbons Jr. (Catholic) and Reverend John N. Samuels-Belboder, the pastor of the African American St. Margaret's Episcopal Church, had filed an injunction to bar the Klan from rallying not only at Memorial Hall but anywhere in the county.

The attorneys who prepared the injunction were active in civic affairs as well as within their respective religious communities: Sidney G. Kusworm, a Jew, and John C. Shea, a Catholic. A county judge granted the injunction hours before the scheduled event. All of this made the front pages of the local dailies. U.S. Supreme Court decisions that would set the bar high for freedom of speech were not yet in place.

Attorney Sidney G. Kusworm. *Courtesy of the Jewish Federation of Greater Dayton.*

Later that year, on its December 9, 1922 front page, the *Dayton Daily* reported on Mayerberg's fiery sermon from the night before at B'nai Yeshurun, in which he challenged Dayton's council of churches to issue a statement condemning the Klan. "The Protestant church has a great opportunity to teach a lesson in vigorous Americanism by condemning this vile un-American organization," Mayerberg declared. The next day, the *Dayton Daily* reported the council's tepid reply: "The Dayton Council of Churches went on record about a month ago as denying certain rumored connections with the Ku Klux Klan….Little more than a month ago, the Federal Council of the Churches of Christ in America issued a statement to the press. It was endorsed by the Dayton Council of Churches officially disclaiming any control over or interest in the Ku Klux movement."

Two Physicians, Two Stories

The stories of physicians Dr. Leo Schram and—a generation later—Dr. Hans Liebermann show how antisemitism grew in Dayton over that period and how the local papers responded. Both of their lives were well covered over several decades in Dayton's dailies.

Wisconsin native Dr. Leo Schram, a Jew, was elected president of the Montgomery County Medical Association (now Society) in 1908. He served as Dayton's city physician for more than two decades, conducting physicals for students in Dayton's public and parochial schools. Schram was the chief medical consultant and on the executive board of Miami Valley Hospital. He was also a member of the Triangle Club, Knights of Pythias and a Mason.

Physician Dr. Hans Liebermann, also a Jew, fled Nazi Germany for America in 1938, passed the Ohio State Board Medical Examination and then arrived in Dayton in 1939. Office buildings refused to rent Liebermann space for his practice, even though occupancy was low at the time. Three hospitals at first rejected his application for privileges, even though he previously had his own ear, nose and throat practice in Germany since 1928. He, along with another Jewish refugee doctor, was rejected for membership in the Montgomery County Medical Association in January 1940—the very society of which Schram was president thirty-two years before.

Liebermann would later recount in an oral history that as soon as the local papers reported on the medical society rejections, new patients showed up at his office to support him. He would go on to assist several hundred Jewish families resettle in Dayton after World War II, and he supplied affidavits for Jewish families to enter the United States.

When I was finishing my book *Jewish Community of Dayton* in 2017, the Montgomery County Medical Society did not know that Dr. Leo Schram had ever served as its president, even though this had been well-documented in Dayton's dailies. It's time to provide the society with this easy-to-confirm information so the good doctor of a century ago will receive the recognition he deserves.

5
AID FOR THE TRANSIENTS

Judaism teaches that all Jews are obligated to give *tzedakah*, to donate righteously to those in need. A Jew is required to give to the poor and the homeless. But what if the person in question is "working the system" or is capable of working and doesn't? What if members of the community are afraid to take in a person in need who might carry disease or lice or suffer from mental illness?

These social welfare dilemmas were at the center of an almost fifty-year struggle among Jewish community leaders over how to service Jewish transients who would come through Dayton for a day or two and then move on to another town. Over the first half of the twentieth century, the rise and fall of the number of transients who came to Dayton reflected the overall shape of the economy, which also affected how much aid local organizations could provide.

Before the establishment of Dayton's Jewish Federation in 1910, Jews in the East End—home of the more recent Jewish immigrants from Eastern Europe—already had a Hachnosis Orchim organization to provide food, lodging and money to transient Jews. The term *hachnosis orchim* refers to the Jewish value of hospitality. By 1912, the federation had approved a motion that stated, "Federation declines to assist any *magid* [itinerant rabbi or teacher] who receives assistance from anyone else in the city and furthermore that no magid should be helped twice." The Jewish Federation made it clear that it was willing to help transient Jews but only if they weren't double-dipping.

The Union Railway Station on West Sixth Street in Dayton. *Courtesy of the Library of Congress.*

In 1915, in the absence of the previous Hachnosis Orchim, the Jewish Federation agreed to continue to care for transients but said it would relinquish the duty of caring for transient magids to a newly forming Hachnosis Orchim in the East End. The Jewish Federation urged the new entity to "cooperate as much as possible and not withhold their contributions from federation."

Also in 1915, Rabbi David Lefkowitz, the chairman of the federation's relief committee, solicited junk dealers and other business owners to give temporary employment to transients. There is no indication that this proposition worked out.

Miriam S. Van Baalen, the executive secretary of the Jewish Federation, expressed her frustration with the transient issue in the federation's 1923 annual report:

> *The transient pursues the same method wherever he goes—that of soliciting the synagogues and business places, while he is being fed and sheltered by the federation, and he often makes it his business to arrive at night so that he will be sure of lodging and have the following day for soliciting* [aid], *rather than working, even if he had the chance.*

The federation provided services to 128 transients that year.

Dayton's Jewish community was not alone in trying to solve this problem. In 1928 and 1929, the National Bureau of Jewish Social Research and more than thirty Jewish organizations around the country studied the issue. At the same time, Dayton's Community Chest looked at the problem of transients in the general community.

The Great Depression brought with it many more transients passing through the city. In 1930, Dayton's Transient Service Bureau was in operation, with lodgings for 81 men. The following year, the Jewish Federation provided 919 transients with care; 548 received a night's lodging, and 371 received cash for food, transportation and incidentals. When Orthodox transient men (mostly elderly) would show up at the Jewish Federation, they weren't sent to the City Transient Bureau; instead, each was given a ticket to stay at a Jewish home. This would ensure kosher meals.

On December 25, 1931, the federation held a meeting at the Jewish Community Center to come to an agreement to curtail duplication of transient services. In the words of Jewish Federation board member Jacob Margolis at the December 25 meeting, "Giving money to a transient only encourages him to become a bum. The thing to do is eliminate that." Federation board member Sam Thal added that "transients discuss these things among themselves, and if the word went around that Dayton took care of them in such a way, the whole town would be flooded with bums."

Present at this meeting was Rabbi I. Rackovsky of the Wayne Avenue (Beth Abraham) Synagogue. He explained that transients first came to the Jewish Federation and then to his synagogue for further assistance. Rackovsky suggested that a committee from the Wayne Avenue Synagogue take over all Jewish transient services and that the Jewish Federation provide the funding. Very often, the rabbi said, transients arrived in Dayton over the weekend, when the Jewish Federation was closed. He also proposed that if a transient wanted more than two meals and a night's lodging, transportation or extra money, that under this new plan, the committee would refer the transient back to the federation.

On January 11, 1932, the executive committee of the federation approved the plan for Rackovsky and Rabbi Samuel Burick of the Wayne Avenue Synagogue to oversee the care of Jewish transients in Dayton who were strict in their observance of dietary laws. All others would be referred to the city's transient service bureau. The Jewish Federation and Wayne Avenue Synagogue agreed not to provide Jewish transients with money.

> Raphael Louis, President
> Louis Ostertag, Treasurer
> Meyer Louis, Secretary

> **Congregation Anshe Emeth**
> Piqua, Ohio January 9 1927
>
> Treasurer's Report 1926
>
> RECEIPTS   EXPENDITURES
>
> CARRIED OVER   ELECTRIC LIGHT   35 67
> FROM 1925   202 96   NATURAL GAS   15 13
> RECEIPTS FROM SEC 524 00   JANITORS   161 05
>   COAL   74 30
> RECEIPTS FROM   PLUMBING   35 56
> MUTUAL INS. CO   9 74   CARPENTER WORK   7 50
>   ASHES HAULED   6 00
>   ELECTRIC GLOBES & WORK 25 23
>   SCHNORRERS (23)   37 30
>   PRAYER BOOKS   5 50
>   TROY PATTERN WORKS   6 00
>   ROOFING   1 00
>   HARDWARE   3 35
>   WATER WORKS   3 75
>   INSURANCE   169 63
>   CEMETERY   91 63
>   ORPHAN ASYLUM   25 00
>   A17. HEBREW UNION   24 00
>   FARM SCHOOL   5 00
>   _____   _____
> $ 736 70 $ 727 55
>
>   BALANCE ON HAND
> $9 15

This 1926 treasurer's report from Congregation Anshe Emeth in Piqua includes an expenditure line for *schnorrers* (Yiddish for moochers), which likely included transients. *Courtesy of Marshall Weiss.*

The number of transients the Jewish Federation serviced in 1932 more than doubled from the previous year to about 1,930. Members of the Wayne Avenue Synagogue—mostly Lithuanian Jews—may have been bolstered in their dedication to carry out this mitzvah by their sense of dignity. The early 1930s brought hard times to the Wayne Avenue Synagogue, too. According to a history of Beth Abraham by Leonard Spialter and Allan Spetter, in June 1931, Rabbis Rackovsky and Burick had not been paid for two months. And the synagogue had difficulty making its mortgage payments. Most congregants couldn't pay their dues.

As the Great Depression ground on, the Jewish Federation softened its stance on giving money to transients; migrants looking for work had joined their ranks.

In a 1975 interview with Renate Frydman for the *Dayton Jewish Chronicle*, Si Burick, the son of Rabbi Samuel Burick, recalled sitting at his parents' dinner table at their home, 40 Bradford Street, with guests he had never met before. "Traveling rabbis, bearded and dressed in the traditional apparel sipped tea and studied Talmud with Rabbi Burick," Frydman wrote. "Their home was one stop on the rounds." Si Burick recalled that at the Jewish Community Center at 59 Green Street, the itinerant travelers took part in daily *minyans* (prayer services) and were given enough money for a ticket to the next town. Rabbi Burick often gave money from his own pocket to see the travelers on their way.

Si Burick's brother, Lee, also recalled in the article that the flow of bearded men to 40 Bradford Street continued long after the Buricks had moved away. As a young man, Lee delivered coal and was called to make a delivery to a new resident at 40 Bradford Street. When he told the woman of the house that he used to live there, she asked him, "Do you know who all these bearded men are who ring my doorbell?"

The Jewish Federation reported that 1,083 Jewish transients, ages ten to seventy-five, including two families, sought aid in 1938. Of these, the Jewish Federation provided 981 men with a small cash allowance for food, and 88 Jewish men accepted a night's lodging at the city transient bureau.

In April 1939, the Jewish Federation convened another meeting to try to centralize and streamline Jewish transient services. Once again, the issues were centered on duplication of services and cash expended. "The transient," Wayne Avenue Synagogue's Philip Kravitz pointed out, "receives cash from both synagogues, from the Hebrew Ladies Benevolent Society and then solicits the businessmen in the city." Kravitz suggested that arrangements be made with a Jewish family to house and

The site of Dayton's Jewish Community Center from 1922 to 1941, 59 Green Street, where itinerant Jews took part in daily minyans and received money. *Courtesy of the Jewish Federation of Greater Dayton.*

feed the transients, that every man coming to the Jewish Federation or the synagogues would receive a ticket for lodging and meals but that no cash be given to him. Sam Thal said it was unfair to subject any family to the care of those men. "Many come in diseased, dirty and their clothes unkept, that no home in Dayton, even if they wanted to house transients, has the proper facilities to take care of them," Thal said.

This time, the Jewish Federation decided to work with all Jewish transients coming to Dayton. They would lodge at the city's transient service bureau; the Jewish Federation would refer Orthodox clients to receive kosher food; and transients were not to receive cash from synagogues or other organizations.

By February 1942, two months after the United States entered World War II, the Jewish Federation reported that both its transient service and the city transient bureau had shown a decrease in the number of people served and monies expended. But at the Jewish Federation's 1942 annual meeting, Executive Secretary Jane Fisher indicated that "a new type of civilian transient is developing—one who seeks employment in defense industries and who is not equipped to meet requirements."

Any mention of transients as an issue of concern is nowhere to be seen in the Jewish Federation's records, brochures or newsletters from the 1950s. By the mid-1960s, the Jewish Federation's Jewish Family Service handled a few transient cases a month, and even that was on the decline: from fifty-nine in 1966 to forty-three in 1970. According to Sheldon Switkin, who served as the director of Jewish Family Service in Dayton from 1982 to 2002, his department handled approximately one dozen transient cases a year during his tenure, keeping confidential records. "A few were 'professional transients,'" he recalled, "but many others were authentic hard luck stories that were verified."

At its centennial in 2010, the Jewish Federation's Social Service Department still handled transient cases, though only about four or five a year. These transients, Jewish men, traveled by bus from city to city, requesting assistance from Jewish federations and synagogue rabbis. Dayton's Jewish Federation provided these transients with bus fare and gift cards to "big box" stores for purchases of essentials. On their way through town, some stayed at hotels overnight, others at homeless shelters.

In recent years, Tara Feiner, the director of Dayton's Jewish Family Services (JFS), said JFS fields requests from Jewish transients once every few years. JFS has referred them to Job and Family Services, food pantries, medical clinics, mental health providers and legal services such as Legal Aid and ProSeniors.

6

THE SPANISH FLU OF 1918–19

"So Many Hearts are Overwhelmed with Sorrow"

On October 4, 1918, Dayton health commissioner Dr. A.O. Peters told the *Dayton Daily News* there was undue alarm about the Spanish influenza outbreak that had hit about 20 people locally. By October 8, Dayton had 168 reported cases. That same day, the Ohio Department of Health laid out closure recommendations, and Peters closed schools, houses of worship and theaters. The next day, he closed saloons, soda fountains and pool rooms. According to the University of Michigan Influenza Encyclopedia, Peters thought the crest of the epidemic had passed, "that Dayton's death rate slowly would return to normal in the coming weeks." As a precaution, though, he would keep the closures in place for another week to ten days. But as adult cases decreased, children's cases increased.

What we know about how the Jewish community was impacted by the pandemic in Dayton in 1918–19 comes to us mainly from the pages of the *Dayton Jewish Life*. Billed as the "First and Only Jewish Paper in Dayton," its editor and publisher was Andrew Roth. The newspaper's run was brief: from the end of 1917 to the end of 1918. Roth may have started the *Dayton Jewish Life* to leverage news stories coming out of the new Jewish Correspondence Bureau, which was reporting on the conditions Jews faced in war-torn Europe. Its editor was Jacob Landau, a twenty-five-year-old journalist in The Hague. The Jewish Correspondence Bureau was soon renamed the Jewish Telegraphic Agency.

The grave of army private Ervin M. Welt at Riverview Cemetery, decorated with a flag placed by Jewish War Veterans Post 587. *Courtesy of Marshall Weiss.*

Dayton Jewish Life covered local news of the Spanish flu in an understated way; not with headline stories on the front page but in society items, news briefs, event listings and a few unsigned editorials. The first Spanish flu item in the *Dayton Jewish Life* appeared in its October 11, 1918 issue: "Dr. A.M. Osness, with offices in the U.B. Building, has been called east to help combat the Spanish influenza epidemic, which seems to have the hardest hold on Boston. On Thursday evening, Dr. Osness left for Boston to be gone until the spread of the Spanish influenza is under control."

Born in Berdichev, Ukraine in the Russian Empire in 1864, Abraham M. Osness arrived in America in 1882. He settled in Dayton to learn the cigar-making trade, according to *Centennial Portrait and Biographical Record of the City of Dayton and of Montgomery County, Ohio*, edited by Frank Conover and published in 1897. Osness attended high school and a commercial college in the city. He received his medical degree in 1894 from the College of Physicians and Surgeons in Chicago and returned to Dayton to open his practice. His wife, Anna K. Osness, would found Dayton's chapter of Hadassah in 1925. The *Dayton Daily News* reported that Osness had volunteered as a consulting physician and was assigned to duty at Pittsfield, Massachusetts, by the government. When Osness returned to Dayton three weeks later, *Dayton Jewish Life* reported, "The time spent there in his effort to get the influenza epidemic under control has proven quite fruitful."

COMFORTING THE BOYS QUARANTINED IN THE CAMPS

The spread of the Spanish flu in America was connected to the movement of soldiers across America and Europe after the United States entered World War I in 1917.

Members of Dayton's chapter of the Jewish Welfare Board—established here in July 1918 to provide support for Jewish and non-Jewish soldiers stationed locally—did their part to help soldiers confined to their quarters under quarantine. "During the time that the Spanish influenza epidemic was at its height at the Wilbur Wright and McCook Fields, the local branch of the Jewish Welfare Board did all in its power to aid in the fight against the epidemic and to save the lives of the boys there," *Dayton Jewish Life* reported on November 1, 1918. "Large quantities of ice cream, crates of oranges and lemons were sent to the field."

The paper also reported in that issue that two of the fatalities at Wright and McCook Fields were Jewish men. "It is with grief and regrets to all, and especially to those who knew them, that Benjamin Goldstein and Ray Goldstein, both of New York and not related, passed into the great beyond." *Dayton Jewish Life* added that Benjamin Goldstein's struggle was "hard but brief," and Ray Goldstein "fought a hard but losing battle for almost a week," and that "his fight attracted the attention of the attendants and his comrades, for no other fought so hard and lost." The October 12, 1918 *Dayton Daily News* reported that Ray Goldstein's father was at his side for twenty-four hours before he died.

A Jewish soldier buried in Dayton who was likely a casualty of the Spanish flu was army private Ervin M. Welt. Born in Cromwell, Indiana, Welt was a jeweler from Schenectady, New York. He was the husband of twenty-three-year-old Leah Jo Moskowitz, the daughter of Dayton's Sallie and Jacob Moskowitz. Leah's father had made his wealth establishing Hungarian labor colonies in Dayton for Malleable Iron Works and Barney and Smith Car Works. The *Dayton Daily News* reported in its January 16,

> **DEATH TOLL AT FIELD NOW 32**
>
> **Three More Soldiers Succumb to Influenza at Wilbur Wright Post. Epidemic Abating.**
>
> Three more deaths in the hospital at Wilbur Wright aviation field Saturday brought the death toll from the influenza epidemic at that post up to 32, all soldiers.
>
> Those whose deaths occurred Saturday were Private Ray Goldstein, New York city; Private James A. Hoag, Petersburg, Va. and Private Vernon Meloney, West Cheshire, Conn.
>
> Major A. G. Farmer, chief medical officer at the field continued to be highly encouraged Saturday evening over the prospects of the epidemic running its course. While there are still some patients at the hospital whose recovery is not expected, the daily falling off in the sick call at the post gives rise to these expectations.
>
> The father of Private Golstein had been at the side of his son for 24 hours before death came.

Dayton Daily News, October 13, 1918. *Courtesy of Cox Enterprises Inc.*

1918 society column that Leah and Ervin had been married the night before in the Moskowitz family home on Lexington Avenue. "The bride's gown was of silver cloth with draperies of silk tulle," the *Daily News* noted. "It was made short, and the tulle veil fell just to the hem. The bodice was of pearl passementerie, and she carried Ascension lilies. Her costume was suited to her brunette beauty, and she looked very sweet and girlish as she took her place to plight her vows."

Ervin enlisted in the army on July 24, 1918. He died of pneumonia—often a complication of the Spanish flu—on October 8, 1918 at Camp Sherman, near Chillicothe, Ohio. The twenty-six-year-old private was buried at B'nai Yeshurun's Riverview Cemetery, next to Joseph Moskowitz, Sallie and Jacob's infant son, who had died in 1900. On Ervin's gravestone is the Hebrew word *mizpah*, literally "watchtower." In Judaism, mizpah signifies the emotional bond between people who are separated.

About seventeen years later, Leah, then living in New York, married actor Harry C. Bannister, the ex-husband of stage and screen star Ann Harding.

According to the National Park Service (NPS), approximately 5,686 cases of influenza were documented among Camp Sherman soldiers in 1918. Of those, 1,777 died. NPS notes that "43,000 U.S. soldiers, around half of those who died in Europe during the war, were killed by the influenza virus and not by a mortal enemy in combat."

Another Spanish influenza death with Dayton connections was that of Captain Arthur Pereles, thirty, who died at his home in Montclair, New Jersey, on October 8, 1918. Born and raised in Dayton, he was the son of Marguerite and Morris Pereles, who owned the London Hat House at 29 East Third Street. Arthur had done well in the importing business. He enlisted in the army after the war broke out and became ill with the flu on September 30, 1918. Arthur was buried in Montclair, leaving behind his wife and two children.

Welt and Pereles are the only known soldiers connected to Dayton's Jewish community to die as part of the Great War. There are 189 known soldiers from Dayton who died in World War I, 85 of them from disease, mostly the Spanish flu.

According to the CDC, the Spanish flu killed 50 million people worldwide, with about 675,000 deaths in the United States. In the few weeks before the Spanish flu's arrival in Dayton, B'nai Yeshurun's rabbi David Lefkowitz, who also chaired Dayton's Red Cross chapter, had put World War I front and center in his Jewish New Year message in the September 7 edition of *Dayton Jewish Life*:

> *In all my 18 years of ministration in this community, none has been as difficult, as full of work as this last year....Never was the community more severely tried than during this selfsame period. And I have not forgotten the flood when I say this, with all its lurid horror and heavy losses. For month after month in the last year, our fine young men have been called from their homes and loved ones, mothers with palpitating hearts bade tearful farewells, and fathers, dry-eyed yet heartstricken, sent their sons to their country's service.*
>
> *The entire community heart was constantly palpitating and fearing and yearning....Along with the rest of the citizens of Dayton, our Jewish people stood the test of patriotism. They gave without stint. They gave their sons. At the present time, 88 Jewish men of Dayton are in the service, many of them enlisted. Forty-one of these are overseas, some in England, but most of them in France. Thirty-eight of the 88 are from Congregation B'nai Yeshurun and the others from Congregation House of Abraham and from Congregation House of Jacob. More men are being called every few weeks, and before October, we shall have over 100 Jewish men from Dayton in the service.*

Jewish Life Society Pages and News Items

Since it began publishing, *Dayton Jewish Life* included announcements on its society page of who was ill and who was recovering from illnesses, though it rarely mentioned what those illnesses were. But with the spread of the Spanish flu epidemic in Ohio in the autumn of 1918, a smattering of announcements began listing the Spanish flu and pneumonia as causes of illness.

The November 1, 1918 *Dayton Jewish Life*, for example, announced, "Corporal Harry Feinberg, stationed at Ohio State University, is recovering from a severe attack of influenza and pneumonia." The same issue listed Herbert D. White, manager of *Dayton Jewish Life*, as being "confined to his home on Lawn Street, suffering from a slight attack of the Spanish influenza." The December 6, 1918 issue informed readers that "the many friends of Mrs. Lester Kusworm will be grieved to learn that she is suffering from the popular malady, la grippe." *La Grippe* was another term used to describe the Spanish flu.

In consultation with the Ohio Department of Health, Dayton Health Commissioner Peters lifted restrictions against public gatherings on November 2, 1918, though schools were still kept closed because of the higher rate of the flu among children. Youths under sixteen were also prohibited from worship services, theaters and libraries. Leaders of Dayton's Talmud Torah, the Hebrew school of Beth Abraham and Beth Jacob synagogues, lamented in the November 1 *Dayton Jewish Life* that though its roster of students had doubled from the previous year, and Talmud Torah superintendent S.B. Maximon had brought an additional Hebrew teacher—Deborah L. Abramson—from New York to Dayton, "the new term's work, already in full swing, has been interrupted by the quarantine."

Peters ultimately opened the schools, only to close grade schools again beginning on December 10, 1918, and continuing through the rest of the year because 20 percent of public school students and 10 percent of parochial school students were absent; approximately 5 percent of students overall had the flu, and parents were afraid to send their children to school.

The worst of the epidemic—according to Peters and Dayton's director of public welfare Dr. Frank D. Garland in their 1919 report—hit the city between October and December 1918, when 657 residents of Dayton died from influenza or influenza-related pneumonia; 44 more people died in the city in January 1919.

Even so, with the ban on public gatherings lifted, Dayton's B'nai B'rith lodge was able to announce in the November 15 *Dayton Jewish Life* that its annual dance, a Chanukah ball which had been scheduled for November 26, was a "sure thing." The Young Men's De Hirsch Club, a Zionist organization, reported that it held a meeting on November 10, its first since the epidemic's closing orders:

> *Many letters from De Hirshites who are in the service were read. This is a real treat to the members and at each meeting, the recipient of letters*

Yiddish theater star Sara Adler performed in Dayton after the city's autumn 1918 public gathering ban was lifted. *Courtesy of the American Jewish Historical Society.*

brings them, and the entire attendance enjoy the contents, which is always a message of good cheer.

B'nai Yeshurun announced that with the closing ban lifted, its children would begin attending classes again the following Sunday, and that "due to the closing order, the plans for a Chanukah entertainment must be changed. As yet nothing definite has been decided upon, but the children may expect a treat as usual."

Yiddish theater star Sara Adler performed in the play *Mothers of the World* in Dayton on November 7 and "won her audience so completely," she presented two more plays in the city over the next few days: *Without A Home* on November 11 and *Broken Hearts* on November 17. With the armistice in place on November 11, several playgoers missed *Without A Home* to participate in Dayton's peace celebration.

"Many people are prone to believe that the Madam Adler in their midst is not the real artist, feeling that Dayton's Jewish community is not large enough to warrant her coming here," *Dayton Jewish Life* reported. "However, the madam wishes to give the Dayton people a treat, realizing that such events as Jewish plays are rare delights here, and for that reason, she has allowed herself to be urged into coming back for a second and even third time."

The Dayton Zionist District held a meeting at the Wayne Avenue Market Hall on November 24 with 350 people in attendance to celebrate the American and Allied victory and the one-year anniversary of the Balfour Declaration, which declared Great Britain's support for a Jewish homeland in Palestine.

Jewish Civilian Deaths

At least three deaths were the direct results of the Spanish flu, and another two likely died from complications of the Spanish flu in Dayton's Jewish civilian population at the time. Of the five, two were buried at Beth Jacob Cemetery, and three were buried at Beth Abraham Cemetery.

Sophia Kauffman was born on July 21, 1892 to Israel and Rose Kaufman in the Russian Empire. She immigrated to the United States in 1907 and found work in Cincinnati as a men's clothing finisher. Israel and Rose arrived in the United States in 1909. Israel became the foreman of a Cincinnati piano factory. Sophia added another "F" to her last name when she married twenty-three-year-old tailor Nathan Kauffman of Dayton on December 9, 1917, in Cincinnati.

Sophia's husband, Nathan Kauffman, was born on February 28, 1895, in the Russian Empire. He arrived in the United States in 1912. On their marriage license, Sophia fudged her age to appear younger, claiming she was twenty-three though she was twenty-five. The couple lived at 1929 East Third Street in Dayton, and she took on the role of housewife.

Sophia died at St. Elizabeth Hospital on October 15, 1918, at the age of twenty-six. She was buried at Beth Jacob Cemetery. Her death certificate records her cause of death as influenza.

The grave of Sophia Kauffman, Beth Jacob Cemetery. *Courtesy of Marshall Weiss.*

Morris Solomon, the son of woodworker Max Solomon of Romania and Leah Cohen Solomon of the Russian Empire, was born on September 2, 1902, in Manchester, England. Max was a cabinetmaker with the Dayton Wright Airplane Company in Moraine. The Solomon family arrived in the United States in 1910 and lived at 1613 East Fifth Street in Dayton. A student, Morris died at home on October 31, 1918, at the age of sixteen. He was also buried at Beth Jacob Cemetery. The cause listed on his death certificate is bronchopneumonia, very likely a result of the Spanish flu.

Buried at Beth Abraham Cemetery was Anna Gorenstein, a housewife, who died at Miami Valley Hospital of bronchopneumonia on October 18, 1918, at the age of thirty-nine. She and her husband, Harry, a salesman, lived at 446 East Fifth Street. Both were born in the Russian Empire, as were their two eldest children. Harry was left to raise their two sons and two daughters: an infant, a toddler and two teenagers. A few years later, he would remarry.

Sam Silberman, who died of influenza at Miami Valley Hospital on December 17, 1918, at the age of fifty-two, was also buried at Beth Abraham Cemetery. Little else is known about this Jew from Russian Poland whose name never appeared in Dayton's city directory. On his death certificate, his occupation is listed as unknown, and his marital status is left empty.

Sarah Berlin, the widow of Nathan Berlin, with their children (*from left to right*): Benjamin, Minnie and Max. *From the collection of Natalie Cohn.*

Fruit peddler Nathan Berlin, born in the Russian Empire, died of influenza at Miami Valley Hospital on October 27, 1918, at the age of twenty-seven. He left behind his wife, Sarah, and their three children—Max, Benjamin and Minnie—all under the age of four, at 229 Allen Street. Nathan Berlin was buried at Beth Abraham Cemetery. "He was helping his uncle—that was Mr. Hyman Schriber—because he was sick, and my grandfather Nathan caught the flu and died," Natalie Cohn of Dayton explained. Natalie is Minnie's daughter; she was named for her grandfather.

Natalie's grandmother Sarah had arrived in the United States in 1914 from Latvia. After Nathan's death, Sarah opened a grocery store with a relative, Samuel Kramer, at 712 South Wayne Avenue. Within a few years, Samuel went back out as a peddler, and Sarah was on her own with the store. "It was a deli, with a pickle barrel and all the deli stuff," Natalie said. As children, Natalie's uncles and mother helped their mother, Sarah, in the store. Natalie said that for a very brief period, her grandmother Sarah remarried. "He was a *shochet* [kosher slaughterer] who lived next door," Natalie said. "He took a liking to my grandmother. My mother didn't like that. Meanwhile, he got her to marry him. That didn't last long."

In the early 1930s, Sarah moved her grocery to the 1900 block of Home Avenue on the West Side. She died in 1944, around the age of fifty, when Natalie was five. "My grandmother was just so sweet and generous," Natalie recalled. "She lived with us upstairs, and she wasn't well. My mother would make a tray of food for my grandmother, and I would take it up to her."

In 1947, Natalie's parents, Minnie and George Rudin, opened the Tropics, a Polynesian-themed nightclub at 1721 North Main Street, which they ran for forty years. Minnie's brothers also worked there.

Spiritual Reflections on the Pandemic and the War

The October 25, 1918 edition of *Dayton Jewish Life* included two unsigned editorials with themes of life and death, well past the High Holy Days:

> *In order to compensate for the discontinuance of public worship, in a number of communities, leaders of respective houses of worship issued a call that the members of their congregations should hold a home service at the hour when the public services are usually conducted....We wonder to*

what extent this old and beautiful custom of Israel was carried out. We wonder whether those of our people who have practically banished religion from their home, grasped the opportunity offered at this time, to make their homes sanctuaries unto God. We wonder whether this terrible scourge will cause them to see the need of giving Judaism the chief place in their lives, in this time of storm and stress, of sickness and perchance death.

The second unsigned editorial told readers:

It is not how long we live, but how we live that counts....In these times, when so many hearts are overwhelmed with sorrow because of the loss of our dear ones, let them ponder deeply over the words of the prophet, and they will find in them the thought that is healing and strengthening. The grief that looks down into the grave will then look up unto the heavens.

7

A HISTORIC ZIONIST CONCERT AT MEMORIAL HALL

"An event of unusual interest is the concert tomorrow evening at Memorial Hall to be given by the famous Palestine chamber music ensemble known as 'Zimro,' which is touring this country in the interest of an art and music temple in Palestine, under the auspices of the Zionist movement," proclaims an article in the December 22, 1919 edition of the *Dayton Daily News*. This "temple" of art and music, the newspaper explained, would be a school for talented young men and women.

The *Dayton Herald* reported that the six members of the ensemble arrived in Dayton on December 22 from Chicago and were on their way to the Hotel Gibbons before they would perform Jewish folk music and Russian peasant songs the next evening. A good night's sleep for these Jewish musicians from Russia was more than warranted. Their journey to America for the tour turned out to be as newsworthy as their concerts.

The musicians of Zimro (Hebrew for music of praise) were clarinetist S. Bellison, a medal winner of the Moscow Conservatory; first violinist J. Mistechkin; violist K. Moldavan; second violinist G. Besrodny; cellist J. Cherniawsky; and pianist L. Berdichevsky—all graduates of the Petrograd Conservatory. When they toured Russia in 1918, on their way to America, they experienced what the *Dayton Daily News* described as "the extremes of fortune."

"They are one of the few artistic organizations who can boast of having actually toured the country at that time, when living conditions were impossible and transportation was even worse," the newspaper reported of

Above: The ensemble Zimro's journey from Eastern Europe to the United States was as newsworthy as its concerts. *From the archives of the YIVO Institute for Jewish Research.*

Left: An advertisement promoting Zimro's concert, *Dayton Daily News*, December 21, 1919. *Courtesy of Cox Enterprises Inc.*

Zimro on December 17, 1919. Their journey played out like one of Sholem Aleichem's tales. Mistechkin said Zimro's accommodations across Russia were, for the most part, freight cars, and they were fortunate if there was room for them to sit on the freight car floor. "Ventilation, there was none, and not infrequently, there was a generous sprinkling of livestock," he added. "The trains crawled along the countryside like slow oxen, sometimes taking five times as long as they should have to reach the destination."

Things were looking up when the group arrived in Perm, Russia, on the day of a labor celebration. Zimro offered to perform for no charge, and "in return, the local soviet granted them a private coach for three weeks, and they traveled 'deluxe.'"

Then, once again, their luck changed for the worse. As reported by George Robinson in the *New York Jewish Week* in 2019, after Zimro journeyed eastward to Russia's Pacific communities, "passing through war zones," they were stranded in Shanghai for six months, waiting for visas to the United States.

Aron Zelkowicz, the founder and director of the Pittsburgh Jewish Music Festival, told Robinson that Zimro was the first proponent of the Russian school of composers "who incorporated East European Jewish folk material into an art music setting." Zimro's tour marked the first time audiences in America would hear Jewish melodies in a classical chamber format. Zelkowicz, himself a cellist, brought musicians with the Pittsburgh Jewish Music Festival to Carnegie Hall's Weill Recital Hall in New York in 2019 for a centennial tribute, a loose recreation of Zimro's sold-out 1919 concert at Carnegie Hall.

Zimro's musicians, staunch Zionists who toured under the auspices of the Central Zionist Organization of Russia, also performed at the American Zionist Federation's convention in Chicago in 1919. In Dayton, Zimro's program opened with the "Star-Spangled Banner" and closed with "Hatikvah," the Jewish national anthem. In between, the audience heard Jewish music arranged for the chamber ensemble by its musicians, including freilachs, wedding music and even "Kol Nidre."

Clarinetist Bellison would become a naturalized citizen after settling in the United States in 1921. He would become first clarinetist with the New York Philharmonic.

ZIONISM IN DAYTON

Zimro's concert in Dayton was sponsored by the Dayton Zionist District, which was established in 1909. That same year, Dayton's Ohave Zion (Love of Zion) Society, then just two years old, reorganized to become an Orthodox synagogue and sought to have its members—and all Zionists in Dayton—purchase land in Palestine to advance Jewish colonization.

In the 1919–20 *American Jewish Yearbook*, Ohave Zion's address was listed as 20 Quitman Street, with 62 memberships and 125 pupils. Ohave Zion even purchased a small portion of Beth Jacob's cemetery for its members. Ohave Zion seems to have faded away by the early 1920s; some of its leaders established the Conservative Dayton View Synagogue Center in 1923. Dayton's two Orthodox synagogues, Beth Abraham and Beth Jacob, visibly supported Zionism. As was the case overall with Reform Judaism at the time, B'nai Yeshurun's members were split on the issue, and its rabbis of the period were not Zionists.

With the collapse of the Ottoman Turkish Empire in World War I, the Balfour Declaration of the British government's support for a Jewish homeland in Palestine on November 7, 1917, and the liberation of Jerusalem by the

Memorial Hall, Dayton, Ohio. *Courtesy of the Dayton Metro Library.*

British on December 9, 1917, Dayton's Zionists exuberantly joined Zionists around the world to do what they could to bring about a Jewish state.

By November 1918, the Dayton Zionist District had about 500 members. Dayton's total estimated Jewish population at the time was 4,500. This support for Zionism came at the same time that Jews in Dayton canvassed to provide aid for the Jews of Europe, who languished in persecution before, during and after World War I.

In February 1919, Cossacks launched a three-day pogrom in the Ukrainian city of Proskurov; 1,500 Jewish residents were murdered. On April 5, 1919, the Polish army executed 35 Jewish residents of Pinsk. Dayton Mayor J.M. Switzer chaired a "strictly non-sectarian" mass meeting at Memorial Hall on June 16, 1919, "for the purpose of voicing the protest of Dayton against the massacre of Jews in foreign lands," the *Dayton Daily News* reported. On December 18, 1919, five days before Zimro's concert, the *Dayton Daily News* ran a report from the Associated Press of a fresh wave of pogroms in the Ukraine, with approximately 5,000 Jews killed in Yekaterinoslav alone.

Four days after Zimro's Dayton concert, Jews and gentiles again filled Memorial Hall to raise $75,000 for the Jewish Relief Campaign. B'nai Yeshurun's rabbi David Lefkowitz and Beth Abraham Synagogue's rabbi Michael Lichtenstein shared the story of the 6 million starving Jews of Europe—800,000 of whom were children—for whom the campaign was conducted. According to the *Dayton Daily News*, Colonel Edward Deeds and the Winters National Bank each donated $1,000 to the cause.

8
JOHN H. PATTERSON, NCR, OAKWOOD AND THE JEWISH COMMUNITY

The city of Oakwood is home to about 160 Jewish households, approximately 10 percent of the Miami Valley's Jewish community. Chabad of Greater Dayton is prominently located there, at the corner of Far Hills Avenue and Grandon Road. Beth Abraham Synagogue, Hillel Academy of Greater Dayton Jewish day school and the Miami Valley Mikvah (ritual bath) are at Sugar Camp, formerly National Cash Register's (NCR) international training center in Oakwood.

Oakwood is an anchor of today's Miami Valley Jewish community, but that was hardly the case a century ago, as I've been reminded from the time I arrived in the Dayton area twenty-five years ago, especially when I was working on the book *Jewish Community of Dayton* a few years back. Before and immediately after the book's publication, I gave several talks about various aspects of the Dayton Jewish community's history. At each Q&A, Jews in our community gravitated toward the same topics: John H. Patterson, NCR, Oakwood and their antisemitism toward the Jews of Dayton. The starting point for all of these discussions was the presumed antisemitism of each.

I only touched on Oakwood's racial restrictions briefly in my previous book. It's a topic worthy of in-depth exploration.

John H. Patterson, born in 1844, was the founder, owner and manager of National Cash Register, which he began in 1884. He is considered the father of Oakwood, which was established as a village in 1908. He died in

Stories of Jewish Dayton

John H. Patterson, the founder, owner and manager of National Cash Register, is also considered the father of Oakwood. *Courtesy of the* Dayton Daily News *Collection, Special Collections and Archives, Wright State University.*

1922. From the era of Patterson's rise with NCR and through his passing, Dayton's Jews fell into two groups. The first to arrive were German Jews, who came to the area in the 1840s because of antisemitism. By the time Patterson was laying the foundations for NCR, Dayton's German Jews were mainly successful merchants who worshiped downtown at the Reform B'nai Yeshurun (now called Temple Israel). Until the flood of 1913, they tended to live in the area of North Robert Boulevard in downtown. They also had their own social club, the Standard Club, not far from B'nai Yeshurun. Beginning in the 1880s, impoverished Jews from Eastern Europe fled to America with the "great wave" of Jewish immigration. They were driven by brutal pogroms and antisemitic restrictions in czarist Russia. In Dayton, they settled in the East End, along Wayne Avenue between Fifth and Wyoming Streets. Jews who came from Lithuania worshiped at Beth Abraham Synagogue; those from everywhere else across the Russian Empire prayed at Beth Jacob Synagogue. For a dozen years, beginning in 1909, an Orthodox Zionist synagogue, Ohave Zion, also met in the East End.

For those who are not too familiar with Patterson, these excerpts from a speech that a community leader gave at the time of his death paint a clear picture of this first citizen of Dayton:

> *He was a passionate lover of his city, raising his voice and spending his effort toward its betterment, the purification of its politics and the beautification of its streets....A true leader of men, he took command on that dark night in Dayton in March 1913, when the levies broke and the waters of the Miami poured into the homes of over half the people of the city. He turned the force of men that he had trained into making cash registers into making boats, one a minute, and then sent them into the waters to feed the marooned population, and to take out to safety the sick and the aged, turning his great factory into a hospital and a refuge.*

Stories of Jewish Dayton

The NCR Factory, as seen from Patterson's Far Hills estate in Oakwood. *Courtesy of the Dayton Metro Library.*

> *But more than that, he will be remembered because of his industrial conscience. He was not willing to degrade his workers to the level of animals and take away their self-respect. So, he pioneered for better factory conditions....He wanted to give his workers a chance to rise, so he educated them, offered them the means to advance....I remember with what joy he spoke to me of the arrangement that he was making for profit-sharing among the workmen. This is John Patterson's monument, this great exemplification of the industrial conscience, his factory. And another would be the city, which he loved with a deep passion.*

The person who said this of Patterson was a Jew: Rabbi David Lefkowitz, who had led B'nai Yeshurun in Dayton from 1900 to 1920. Lefkowitz gave this sermon from his new pulpit at Temple Emanu-El in Dallas.

This was the same John H. Patterson whose management team, at least in America, was all-White and generally Protestant. A natural outgrowth was the village of Oakwood, an idyllic haven for Patterson and his executives, welcome only to White Christians.

The historic record is full of surprising contradictions. In the public square, Patterson did work with leaders in Dayton's Jewish community. And the public country club he gave to the city of Dayton was open to all of its citizens in some form or another. But the legacy of his prejudices and how racial restrictions played out at NCR and in Oakwood linger in the collective memory of Dayton's Jews. This has even led to local legends about Patterson and the Jews—stories that are not factually or historically correct but offer those who pass them on some imagined justice against racial restrictions.

Here is what we know from the historical record.

Advancement for Some

Black Americans were hired at NCR—at least in the beginning—as janitors and in the foundry. Jews were able to work in the factory and in clerical positions. Along with photographic evidence of Black Americans at NCR are two letters—written in 1904 and 1905—from S.J. Gorman, the foreman of NCR's janitors. In both, Gorman wrote, "My janitor force are all colored men and there are 75 of them."

Mark Bernstein, the author of *Grand Eccentrics—Turning the Century: Dayton and the Inventing of America* (1996), told me that Patterson thought of NCR as a meritocracy. But at the same time, Patterson's version of logic led him to eliminate his Black employees. "He believed every employee could rise to the top," Bernstein said. "At one point, he concluded that since White employees would not work for a Black supervisor, Blacks could not be promoted and, therefore, had no real future with the company. So, he fired them. My best guess is that this involved about 200 Black employees out of a total labor force of 5,000 to 6,000. My best view is that this happened sometime between 1905 and 1910."

In a 1985 oral history project the Jewish Federation of Greater Dayton facilitated, one participant, Charlie Froug, talked about his father, Israel Froug, and uncle Charlie Vangrov. In 1913, both were carpenters in Cincinnati. When the flood hit Dayton that year, Israel Froug and Charlie Vangrov came from Cincinnati for two weeks to work at NCR, initially building boats. The two thought Dayton was the most beautiful city they had ever seen. Israel Froug went to work for NCR in 1915. Charlie Froug recalled of his father, Israel:

> *He was fired the first week he was there. He was shomer Shabbos* [Sabbath observant]. *He wouldn't work on the Sabbath and was given a pink ticket*

when he came back on a Monday. He was wild that day and went to John H. Patterson and called him an anti-Semite, with his real honest-to-God Yiddish accent. John H. was upset and wanted to know why. He told him, "I didn't come to work on Saturday: that's my Sabbath. I'll work on your Sabbath if you'll keep the plant open." Patterson made a deal. If he could make the number of pieces in the five days that the other men did in six, he didn't have to come in on Saturdays.

Israel Froug accepted.

Before Russian-Polish Jew Benjamin Shaman became a prominent attorney in Dayton, his first job after he graduated Stivers High School in 1909 was as a stenographer for NCR.

Bruce W. Ronald and Virginia Ronald wrote in *Oakwood: The Far Hills* (1983) that before the turn of the twentieth century, Patterson built the Far Hills, his summer home, on the shade-covered hills of what would become the village of Oakwood:

Patterson's paternalism began to spread to Oakwood. First, he encouraged his executives to move there. Later, Patterson would encourage his foremen

Patterson's Far Hills estate in Oakwood, just south of Dayton. *Courtesy of the Dayton Metro Library.*

to move to Oakwood as well. His method of enticing people to the village was simple. With the terms available, his employees could not afford to live elsewhere. The overall price was low, the down payment practically non-existent and the monthly payments negligible.

Patterson made this possible when he contracted the John B. Stetson Building and Loan Association of Philadelphia to serve as the building and loan association for NCR employees. The arrangement was proclaimed in the July 1898 *American Building Association News*.

This building and loan association had been established in 1880 by legendary hatmaker John B. Stetson for his factory employees, to help them "in building their own homes and to encourage them in saving money for that purpose and for the benefit of their families."

Gorman's letters from 1904 and 1905 inform us that NCR's building association was not used by the "working men and women at the factory." Rather, they "don't live, and won't, in any particular district. They prefer neighborhoods which they select themselves for their own reasons, and they prefer houses built in such places, and such ways, as suit the individual taste." The foreman continued:

> *There has never been any inquiry whatever from the company as to how these men live or where. The men prefer to take care of themselves, and are able to, in the matter of housing, and in their own way. They need no assistance from the company on the subject. The building associations in Dayton are many; they are all, or nearly all, very good.*

It's not known whether this arrangement of Stetson building association use exclusively for NCR executives and foremen was according to Patterson's design or if that's just how it worked out.

When Oakwood had enough residents to incorporate as a village in 1908, Patterson's name was at the top of the incorporation documents. "Once he got into his head to plan for the future of Oakwood, there was no aspect of the community that didn't bear his mark or receive his advice," wrote Joanne K. McPortland in *Oakwood, From Acorn to Oak Tree: A Centennial Celebration 2008.*

Racial Residential Restrictions

It wasn't until after the Great Dayton Flood of 1913 that Oakwood experienced growth as a "high and dry" community for Dayton's well-to-do citizenry. And Oakwood didn't truly boom until the 1920s.

Before the flood, Dayton's fashionable set lived along Robert Boulevard, which followed the contour of the Miami River's east bank downtown. The emerging affluent suburbs on high ground were Dayton View and Oakwood, both accessible by a trolley line.

Those familiar with Dayton's Jewish history know that discriminatory real estate restrictions kept Jews from living in Oakwood. Jews with the means to do so moved to Dayton View, and some led the way there in the years before the flood. There's even documentation that the Wright family—which had initially purchased land in March 1910 for a new home at Salem Avenue and Harvard Boulevard in Dayton View—ultimately decided to build its house at Harman and Park Avenues in Oakwood, at least in part out of concern that Jews were moving to Dayton View.

On May 7, 1911, Orville Wright wrote in a letter to his brother Wilbur that a soon-to-be neighbor of theirs on Harvard Boulevard had advertised in that morning's *Dayton Journal* that he was selling his property. "We are afraid it will be sold to some friend of our conspicuous Hebrew neighbors," Orville wrote. This was in addition to design challenges they encountered because of the size of the lot. Katharine Wright, Orville and Wilbur's sister, wrote to family friend Griffith Brewer on November 8, 1911, "I think Will and Orv are very glad we did not go ahead on the original lot. Many things are making that neighbourhood rather undesirable."

What exactly were the racial restrictions south of Dayton, and how did they play out? Two ways to put racial housing restrictions on lots in Montgomery County were to include them at the plat level or at the deed level.

The first discriminatory real estate restrictions in Montgomery County were recorded at the plat level in Van Buren Township; the township no longer exists. Parts of Van Buren Township became Oakwood beginning in 1908, and the remainder became Kettering (1952) and Moraine (1953). Montgomery County's first plat with discriminatory restrictions was recorded as approved by the county on October 6, 1924, "in accordance with the rules and regulations adopted by the director of public service of the City of Dayton, Ohio, acting as supervisor of plats." Though this plat was in Van Buren Township, not Oakwood (today, it's in Dayton), the developers capitalized on the marketing appeal of Oakwood in the plat's name, McKnight's East Oakwood Plat.

The developers and their lender, the Permanent Building and Savings Association, received approval for the platting with the restriction: "That in consideration of the price at which property is sold the said purchaser agrees not to sell, transfer, lease or rent said property to any person other than of the Caucasian race." This language excluded Jews. White America, at that time, didn't consider Jews or Italians to be Caucasians.

In the 1920s, the pseudoscience of "eugenics"—the racist pursuit of scientific proof of inferior and superior races championed by Anglo-Protestants in academia—rose to its peak of influence in America. The U.S. Congress used it as a pretext to curtail immigration from Eastern Europe (Jews) and Southern Europe (Italians) by 87 percent beginning in 1924. The U.S. State Department recorded that the purpose of the Immigration Act of 1924 was "to preserve the ideal of U.S. homogeneity."

Nazi Germany would take eugenics "research" developed in the United States and run with it. Such national immigration restrictions kept the Jews of Eastern and Central Europe trapped in the Holocaust. "The late 19th and early decades of the 20th century saw a steady stream of warnings by scientists, policymakers, and the popular press that 'mongrelization' of the Nordic and Anglo-Saxon race—the real Americans—by inferior European races (as well as by inferior non-European ones) was destroying the fabric of the nation," Karen Brodkin wrote in *How Jews Became White Folks & What that Says About Race in America* (1998). She added that, for Jews, "this picture radically changed after World War II," when they were more generally accepted as "model middle-class White suburban citizens."

Two plats in Montgomery County carried racial restrictions in 1927. The Wellmeiers Oakwood Plat in Dayton reads, "No lot or residence building on this plat shall be conveyed, leased, rented or occupied by persons other than of the White Race"—language put into place by Wellmeiers Brothers Realty Company. The third section of McKnights East Oakwood Plat, then in Van Buren Township (now Dayton), employed the same restrictive language as the first. The second platted section didn't include racial restrictions.

Two other plats in Van Buren Township in 1928 included racial restrictions. Both read:

> Each grantee of a lot or lots on this plat—for himself, his heirs, executors, administrators, and assigns agree that he will not sell, assign to or create a lien by mortgage or otherwise in favor of any person of any but the

Caucasian race or blood; that no person of any other race or blood shall become a purchaser or assignee or become entitled to the possession thereof.

In Oakwood, investors and developers didn't place racial restrictions on residential real estate at the plat level; they put them at the deed level. This was because the U.S. Supreme Court had struck down racial zoning ordinances in 1917 (*Buchanan v. Warley*), but it upheld the legal right of property owners to enforce racially restrictive covenants in 1926 (*Corrigan v. Buckley*). But as Richard Rothstein points out in *The Color of Law: A Forgotten History of How Our Government Segregated America* (2017), many border and Southern cities simply ignored the Buchanan decision.

Those looking for a more airtight legal procedure would have opted to place racial restrictions at the deed level.

At the beginning of 2020, Tina S. Ratcliff, the Montgomery County Records and Information manager, and Amy Czubak, a technician with Montgomery County Records Center and Archives, began to search for deeds with racial restrictions in Oakwood to aid my research. With Ratcliff's guidance, Czubak found ten examples. "The plats we included are from 1872 to 1937," Czubak said of the search. "There are only eight plats that were created pre-flood, and none of them had racial restrictions." She added that she and Ratcliff were "95-percent sure" they had looked at deeds in all of Oakwood's plats for that timeframe. She surveyed sixty-eight plats in total. Czubak looked at the restrictions on the first deed for each plat. "I don't think that this is in every single plat in Oakwood," she said. "It's 1924 to 1933 where you get this big influx. It wasn't all of Oakwood. It seems like it was almost a little corner of Oakwood that was just trying to keep everybody out that wasn't considered some sort of Caucasian." Czubak described some of the deeds as "quite extraordinary." "There are a few that specifically mention no Chinese, Japanese or Negroes, and one that specifically states the property cannot be leased, rented or sold to anyone of Ethiopian descent," she said.

In 1924, the seller of a lot in the Anna M. Neibel Plat in Van Buren Township included in the deed that "said premises shall not be sold, transferred, leased or rented to any person of Negro descent." This plat was annexed into Oakwood in 1926. The Stomps Realty Company included racial restrictions at the deed level for three lots it sold in 1925 within the Oakwood View Plat, also located in Van Buren Township. This deed specified "that none of this property shall be sold, leased or rented to anyone of African descent." This plat was also part of the 1926 annexation into Oakwood. And the seller of a lot in the Far Hills East Plat in Van Buren Township—another plat that would be annexed into Oakwood in 1926—included in the 1925 sales deed that "said premises shall not be sold, transferred, leased or rented to any person or persons not of the Caucasian race."

The first known racial deed restriction that originated in Oakwood dates to January 12, 1928, with a lot in the Far Hills Estate First Edition Plat. The deed states, "No persons of Ethiopian blood shall be permitted to purchase, lease or occupy any lot in this subdivision." Only one day later, the deed for the sale of a lot in the Mahrt Estate Plat in Oakwood included the restriction: "That this property shall not be sold, transferred, leased, rented or permitted to be occupied by any person or persons other than members of the White race." Restrictions in 1929 on five lots in the Neibel Park Addition Plat in Oakwood indicate on the deed that "said premises shall not be transferred, leased or rented to any person or persons not of the Caucasian race."

The City National Bank Trust Company of Dayton, acting as trustee in 1929, sold one and a half lots in the Elizabeth Gardens Plat in Oakwood and one lot on the plat of the Village of Oakwood, with a restriction on the Elizabeth Gardens lots that "at no time shall any of the land…or any building erected thereon be occupied by any person of Negro, Chinese or Japanese extraction; but this prohibition is not intended to include or prevent occupancy by such person or persons as domestic servants or while employed in or about the premises by the owner or occupant of any land included in said plat."

The Caldwell and Taylor Corporation purchased three lots in the Mary Knoll Plat in Oakwood in 1931; they included the restriction, "Said premises shall not be sold, transferred, leased or rented to any person or persons not of the Caucasian Race."

The largest and latest of Czubak's finds dates to 1933. The same family that sold a lot in the Anna M. Neibel Plat (1924) and five lots in the Neibel Park Addition Plat (1929) sold thirty-six lots in the Far Hills East Plat in Oakwood with the restriction: "Said premises shall not be sold, transferred, leased or rented to any person or persons not of the Caucasian Race."

Czubak said that, overall, there aren't that many deeds with racial restrictions in Montgomery County. "I still get surprised when I come across one," she said. "It's not so commonplace that when I open up a deed all I think of is there's going to be another one. There's no specific place or area in Dayton. It's spread out." Although she added: "Ten deeds is a pretty large amount all for one little village at the time."

An Era of Antisemitism

The 1920s and 1930s marked the worst period for mainstream antisemitism in United States history. In 1920, Henry Ford attempted to further inflame Jew hatred through his *Dearborn Independent* newspaper, which he also distributed at all Ford dealerships. Ford had the most virulent antisemitic articles from his newspaper compiled and published in four volumes for his anthology series, *The International Jew*.

The Second Ku Klux Klan—established in 1915 on Stone Mountain in Georgia—made its presence known in Dayton on Monday, August 15, 1921, according to an article in the *Dayton Daily News*. "Secret but impressive ceremonies are said to have marked the meeting on Monday night of the Klan in Timmer's Woods, along the Lebanon Pike (now Far Hills Avenue), south of Dayton, when seven new members were inducted into the hooded order," the *Dayton Daily News* reported on August 19, 1921. "Membership of the organization Friday was said to number about 40, many of whom are prominent citizens of Dayton. Their names have not been made public." The article continued, "It was reported Friday the local Ku Klux Klan has been formed by a local manufacturer and organizers from Cincinnati and Atlanta…[and that] the manufacturer, who is said to head the Klan here, is said to be a resident of Oakwood."

The *Daily News* also reported that the Klan distributed printed cards in Dayton bearing its principles. Among those were: "Shielding the chastity of your pure womanhood…eternal maintenance of white supremacy; upholding and preservation from tyrannical oppression from any source whatsoever, of those sacred constitutional rights and privileges of a free-born Caucasian race of people, so wisely enacted by the founders of our constitution."

The Klan's targets in Dayton, as elsewhere, were Black people, Catholics and Jews. The Klan burned crosses in neighborhoods where their targets lived, including—as documented in the *Dayton Daily News*—one on the Dover Street Hill in Dayton's East End Jewish neighborhood in March 1923.

In August 1923, the *Dayton Daily* reported that "approximately 20,000 members of the Ku Klux Klan assembled at Forest Park…said to be the largest meeting of the organization ever held in the city." By 1924, Dayton's Klan had at least 15,000 members, according to University of Dayton professor Bill Trollinger, an authority on the Klan in Ohio who teaches history and religion courses.

The absence of racial restrictions on plats or deeds in Montgomery County before 1924 comes as no surprise to Janet Bednarek, a professor and

Dayton's Knights of the Ku Klux Klan "Klonclave," September 21, 1923, with seven thousand members in attendance. *Courtesy of the Dayton Metro Library.*

former chair of the history department at the University of Dayton. "Deed restrictions are an old tool, but before the twentieth century [were] used primarily to try to control 'noxious' uses—slaughterhouses, tanneries, etc.," Bednarek, who specializes in urban history, explained.

> *It was only in the twentieth century—largely in the wake of the mass immigration of the late nineteenth century and, even more so, the Great Migration of African Americans—that they were used to try to control the race/ethnicity of urban/suburban neighborhoods.*
>
> *The 1920s seems to be the decade that these became widely used. Oakwood, essentially, was created to deliberately separate its residents from the city of Dayton. Undoubtedly, the residents did not want any number of "undesirables" to "infiltrate" their community.*

"Likely, they were more unwritten," Bednarek said of racial restrictions in Oakwood before 1924.

> *Most people have a sense of the "social geography" of their cities—where they are welcome or not. Realtors and banks would be aware of this social*

geography as well. There probably weren't any written restrictions on African Americans or on certain ethnic groups (Poles, Hungarians, etc.) common in Dayton. Further, most servants at this time were still White, so people in Oakwood would not be concerned about the race of live-in servants yet either—as they would be once more African Americans became servants in homes in the 1920s following immigration restrictions.

She also pointed out that home ownership wasn't yet the mass phenomenon it would be after World War II. "Not even a majority of the middle class owned their own home," Bednarek said. "It was a very expensive proposition. Given Oakwood's origins as an NCR/corporate enclave, the makeup of the population who could afford to move there in the first place was fairly restrictive to begin with."

Economic restrictions found on plats in Oakwood beginning in the 1920s excluded those of lesser means, many of whom were not White or considered White. Those restrictions often specified that only a single home could be built on a lot and that the home would have to be valued at least at a certain price.

Bednarek said the reason 1924 was the first year racial restrictions appeared on deeds in Montgomery County is explained in a book published in 2020, *Segregating the Suburbs: Developers and the Business of Exclusionary Housing, 1890–1960*, by Paige Glotzer. One chapter details how developers spread information about how to use covenants to restrict suburban developments in the United States.

"One key player was the Roland Park Company of Baltimore," Bednarek said. The company, which had developed restrictive racial covenants in the 1890s, began to disseminate information on how to use such covenants by 1913. Bednarek said:

> *Initially, the dissemination mostly involved key members of the Roland Park Company talking to the few other big suburban developers in the U.S.… However, the company was also a key member of the National Association of Real Estate Boards* [NAREB]. *It turned out that NAREB became the vehicle used to disseminate information on covenants more widely. The author of the book states that the 1920s was the key decade in which the idea of covenants spread nationally as a result of the work of the NAREB.*

The NAREB, Bednarek said, issued a publication in 1923 that included this information.

"So, why 1924? That might be when the information of how to use the covenants to restrict suburbs made it to Oakwood's realtors," she said.

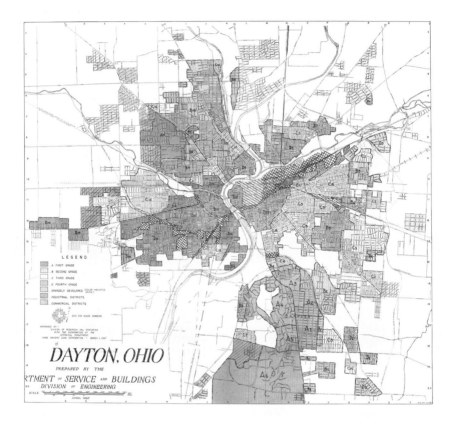

The Home Owners' Loan Corporation Residential Security Map of Dayton in 1937 brought redlining here. *Courtesy of the Library of Congress.*

THE BIRTH OF REDLINING

Bednarek also pointed out the Home Owners' Loan Corporation (HOLC) Residential Security Map of Dayton from 1937.

President Franklin D. Roosevelt established HOLC in June 1933 with congressional approval. Its aim was to refinance mortgages in default as well as prevent future foreclosures at a time when home ownership was still not within the reach of most Americans. But HOLC also created the racial inequity of "redlining."

In 1935, the Federal Home Loan Bank Board had HOLC draw up "residential security maps" for 239 cities across the United States. The maps color coded each city's neighborhoods and suburbs based on the security and risk assessments of real estate investments in those locations.

Each color represented an investment grade. The stated purpose of the maps was to "graphically reflect the trend of desirability in neighborhoods from a residential viewpoint." The less desirability, the less likely the federal government would be to provide loan insurance to government-approved lenders. Factors HOLC considered in its assessments included "social status of the population." Along with HOLC field agents, each local map was prepared in collaboration with members of the city's real estate board. This was the case in Dayton.

Grade A classifications, colored green, were considered the best real estate investments in a city. At the very bottom were grade D areas, considered the riskiest in which to grant mortgages. Grade D areas were colored red. One of the great risk factors HOLC assigned to suburbs or neighborhoods was the amount of "infiltration" of "undesirables," essentially those not considered White, and the poorest of the White population.

Redlining perpetuated the difficulties of those in the Black American community in securing reasonable mortgage terms—if they could secure mortgages at all. It kept them in housing that would become overcrowded, substandard and ghettoized in the neighborhoods where they were allowed to live.

Dayton's 1937 HOLC map gives a snapshot of the racial restrictions that were in place across the Dayton area when redlining had just begun, particularly through the details listed on HOLC area description forms for each location. All of the forms included lines for agents to fill out for favorable and detrimental influences, as well as percentages of foreign born, "Negro," "infiltration of" and "relief families."

Out of a total of forty-six areas on the 1937 Dayton HOLC map, only seven areas achieved grade A classifications; five of them were in sections of Oakwood. The five Oakwood area description forms essentially read the same. Always listed on the lines for favorable influences were "restricted" or "highly restricted." On each grade A form for Oakwood, there were no listings of foreign born, "Negro," "infiltration of" or "relief families." The sixth grade A area listed was in Van Buren Township, south of Oakwood. The word "restricted" didn't appear in the area description, though neither did any foreign born, "Negro," "infiltration of" or "relief families." Another "highly restricted" area, though with a grade B rating, was the section straddling Dayton and Oakwood, close to the NCR plant.

Only one other neighborhood received a grade A ranking in the Dayton area in 1937, and it was listed as "highly restricted." It may surprise Jews in our community to learn that it was Upper Dayton View.

A dozen years later, all of Dayton's Jewish congregations would be located in Dayton View, and the majority of Dayton's 5,500 Jews essentially lived within a one-mile radius of the congregations. That a portion of Dayton View was once restricted to Jews isn't commonly remembered today. A 1924 deed for a lot sold by the Schwind Realty Company in the Upper Dayton View Development Company Plat, for example, had a Whites-only restriction.

By 1937, Dayton's Jewish community had migrated from the East End; Jews had settled in Lower Dayton View in two areas. Twenty percent of the residents in the area just south of Upper Dayton View were listed as Italian and Jewish on the lines "foreign born" and "infiltration of." This area held a grade B designation, comprising single- and double-family homes in which 40 percent were homeowners.

Just south of that area, still in Lower Dayton View, was another neighborhood where Jews lived, bearing a grade C-. The form listed this location's inhabitants as 80 percent "Russian Jewish, German-Polish," with an "infiltration of foreign-Jewish…centering in this area."

On the 1937 Dayton HOLC map, another eight areas were listed as restricted: four more in Van Buren Township, three more in Dayton and one straddling Dayton and Madison Township.

Exceptions to the Rules

Three Jewish families did live in Oakwood when they weren't supposed to.

The first was women's clothing merchant Joseph Thal, his wife, Pearl, and their children. Joseph Thal was born in Dayton in 1886 and Pearl Thal was born in Columbus in 1889, both to parents from Galicia (between Central and Eastern Europe). The Thals are first listed as living in Oakwood at 825 Far Hills Avenue in the *1918 Williams' Dayton City Directory*. Their son Norman graduated from the new Oakwood High School. But the family moved to 1116 Harvard Boulevard in Lower Dayton View by the time the 1926 Dayton city directory was in print.

Next were optometrist Joseph T. Cline and his wife, Harriette, who were first listed as living at 82 East Dixon Avenue in Oakwood in the 1923 Dayton city directory. Cline was born in Wales in 1893 and was raised in Birmingham, England. His wife was born in 1893 in Pennsylvania to parents who were from Hungary and Germany. Joseph T. Cline arrived in the United States in 1914. A year later, he worked in the Elder & Johnston Company department store's optical department. In 1917, he opened his own practice in Downtown Dayton.

Cline became John H. Patterson's optometrist. In his memoirs, Cline described Patterson as "an anomaly to me, a gentle, good-natured person, charitable and considerate of others, yet ruthless in his treatment of competitors," adding that "he was extremely harsh with employees he deemed to be inefficient. He could not tolerate 'yes men' and showed appreciation of those employees who stood up to him."

Cline wrote that Patterson's valet, "Roberts," brought his young son to see him for an eye exam. The optometrist fitted Roberts's son with glasses, and the boy did much better at school. The valet convinced Patterson to consult Cline. "Roberts informed me that his employer had suffered for years with headaches, which his physician insisted was due to eye strain," Cline wrote. "Patterson constantly visited ophthalmologists in the U.S. and Europe who had been recommended to him, but he still suffered with severe headaches. Roberts brought him to me for an eye examination. It immediately was evident that his glasses could be the cause of the headaches."

Cline wrote he was able to correct Patterson's prescription and another problem that was causing him headaches. "He had a habit of pulling his glasses off his nose and pounding them in his fist, to emphasize a point. I insisted on prescribing rigid spectacles that could not easily get out of alignment. He demurred and said, 'Make the lenses and put them into one of my old nosepieces.'" Cline said he angrily told him, "Mr. Patterson, I would take your advice in selecting a cash register for my needs, and I expect you to take my advice

Joseph Thal. *Courtesy of the Dayton Daily News Collection, Special Collections and Archives, Wright State University.*

Joseph T. Cline. *From the collection of Meredith Cline.*

as to eyeglasses. Either you will do so, or you may look for another eye-examiner." At this, Cline reported that Patterson burst into laughter and said, "Why did not other eye-men talk to me like that? Go ahead and do it your way."

After wearing his new glasses for a few days, Patterson dropped in to express his satisfaction and selected fourteen different styles of frames, two of each kind, for a total of twenty-eight pairs. Cline wrote:

> *From then on, there was hardly a day without some elderly person, one of his employees, or some hobo he picked up on the street, presenting one of Patterson's cards authorizing an eye-examination and glasses to be charged to him. He suggested that I establish an office at his factory and examine the eyes of all of the thousands of his employees, but I was too busy with my regular practice.*

After the Clines moved to Oakwood—during the last year of Patterson's life and not far from his estate—Patterson frequently asked his optometrist to come to his home with optical pliers and adjust his glasses. Patterson continued pounding his glasses on tables to emphasize a point. At times, Cline wrote that he found all twenty-eight pairs of Patterson's glasses required alignment. "I spent many hours in discussion with him, but conversation always got back to cash registers," Cline wrote. "No person before or since has done so much for the city of Dayton than Patterson."

The Cline family lived in Oakwood for seventeen years; their children went to school from kindergarten through high school there. Harriette and Joseph T. Cline then moved to 1053 Cumberland Avenue, on the only nonrestricted block of that street in Lower Dayton View. Cline's last word about Oakwood in his memoirs: "A splendid place to raise youngsters."

A third Jewish family who lived in Oakwood early on was the Kohnops. Max Kohnop and his wife, Minnie, were first listed as living at 236 Monterey Avenue in the 1927 Dayton city directory. At the time, Max Kohnop was the assistant city editor at the *Dayton Daily News* and the local correspondent for the Associated Press.

Born in Cincinnati in 1898 to parents who had emigrated from the Russian Empire, Kohnop had moved to Dayton with Minnie in 1922, when the *Dayton Daily News* hired him away from the *Cincinnati Enquirer*. From 1939 to 1964, he served as the Sunday editor of the *Dayton Daily News*. And from 1934 to 1976, Kohnop was president of Oakwood's

Max Kohnop. *Courtesy of the Dayton Daily News Collection, Special Collections and Archives, Wright State University.*

Wright Library Board; he would serve on the board until 1981. He was known as the father of the Wright Library.

Kohnop brought to fruition Oakwood's decades-old dream of having its own library building. He guided the library through its greatest periods of growth, when its levy was passed in 1938 and the new building opened and through expansions in 1964 and 1972.

Because Kohnop served as the president of the Oakwood Library Board, he became one of very few to get as close as anyone could to the extremely guarded introvert and Oakwood resident Orville Wright. Kohnop already knew Wright from the days when he covered aviation. When a vacancy came open on the library board around 1937–38, someone suggested Orville Wright for the position. It was Kohnop who called Wright and asked him to join the board. Wright agreed to serve as the vice president, with two conditions: one, that he would never be quoted in the newspaper, with everything he said off the record, and two, that Wright would never have to preside over a meeting.

Sandy Senser of Columbus, the granddaughter of Minnie and Max Kohnop, doesn't recall them talking about why they moved to Oakwood or about the discrimination they may have faced there. "They kept kosher, they kept to themselves," Senser said.

> *They were neighborly, they had good neighbors, but you just didn't make a big deal about being Jewish. They would eat out, but they would only eat fish. I don't recall going to shul* [synagogue] *with them, partly because Grandpa worked on Saturday, working on the Sunday edition....He used to come home at 2 in the morning or something like that after the paper was put to bed. She* [Minnie] *always lit Shabbos candles, we celebrated the holidays.*

The Thals, Clines and Kohnops were active in the general and Jewish communities in very public ways. They were also all members of Dayton's Reform Jewish congregation, B'nai Yeshurun.

Patterson and Rabbi Lefkowitz

In the public square and for the good of the Dayton community as a whole, Patterson worked with Jewish leaders. His closest Jewish relationship seems to have been with Rabbi David Lefkowitz, who eulogized him from Dallas in 1922.

Born in Hungary and orphaned in New York, Lefkowitz served Dayton's B'nai Yeshurun from 1900 to 1920. He was a remarkable leader and social justice champion in Dayton's Jewish and general communities. He absorbed German Jewish Reform values at the Hebrew Orphan Asylum in New York and from Rabbi Isaac Mayer Wise at Hebrew Union College (HUC) in Cincinnati, where he was ordained. Lefkowitz brought Jews from across Dayton together and brought the Jewish and general communities closer together, too.

The rabbi had received a bachelor of science degree at City College in New York and taught there for two years. He also studied at the Art Students' League. Lefkowitz graduated Phi Beta Kappa from the University of Cincinnati while attending HUC. His wife, Sadie Braham, came from a family of English Jews who had immigrated to Cincinnati. They were married in 1901. Together, their embrace of arts and culture charmed gentile Daytonians.

David Lefkowitz became an active member and speaker with the Saturday Evening Club, a long-running discussion salon in Dayton. "About 1,000 people enjoyed a genuine old German evening at the Allen School," the *Dayton Daily News* reported in 1911. "Rabbi David Lefkowitz delivered an interesting address supplemented with stereopticon views of German scenes, and Mrs. Lefkowitz rendered a number of German songs."

Reverend Augustus Waldo Drury wrote of David Lefkowitz in his 1909 *History of the City of Dayton and Montgomery County*, "He does not feel any narrow racial or sectarian boundaries but is a man of broad humanitarian spirit and who has been a close student of the vital questions of the day." Virtually no progressive social cause went forward in Dayton without the rabbi's leadership.

In 1907–8, Lefkowitz chaired the Dayton Citizens' Relief Committee to assist the unemployed. In 1910, he founded the Jewish Federation of Greater Dayton. He also served on the first executive committee of the Dayton NAACP when it was established in 1915. He was the vice president of the Montgomery County Humane Society (which prevented cruelty to people as well as animals then), the vice president of the Dayton Vacation School Association, the chairman of the Dayton Playground

Sadie and Rabbi David Lefkowitz's embrace of arts and culture charmed Dayton's gentile community. *Courtesy of the Temple Emanu-El Archives, Dallas.*

Committee and a member of the educational committee of the Dayton Chamber of Commerce.

In 1917, with America's entry into World War I, the president of B'nai Yeshurun, Ferdinand Ach (also the Jewish Federation's first president), served as temporary chair of Dayton's then-forming Red Cross. Ach focused on civilian relief work, along with Katharine Wright and Patterson. When the local Red Cross asked Patterson to become its first permanent chair, Patterson declined. The committee turned to Lefkowitz as its chair, to oversee the mobilization of volunteer committees that provided much-needed medical supplies and nursing care for U.S. soldiers in Europe. After the war, Lefkowitz led the chapter in its transition to local services for those in need, and the comfort and welfare of returning soldiers. It's unlikely Ach and Lefkowitz would have received these leadership positions with the Red Cross without Patterson's approval.

There are numerous examples of Patterson opening opportunities for the Jewish community in the public sphere.

In 1907, the Dayton Chamber of Commerce was born when Patterson demanded that Dayton establish one or he would leave the city and take NCR with him. The chamber's second president, from 1908 to 1911, was Bavarian-born Jew Leopold Rauh, who owned the Egry Register Company. Rauh served on Dayton's board of education and on the commission that established Dayton's city manager form of government, another key project of Patterson.

At the same time that Oakwood was essentially restricted racially, Patterson made recreational amenities elsewhere available to all members of the broader community. When Patterson opened his Hills and Dales Country Club over Memorial Day Weekend in 1916, it was billed in advertisements in the *Dayton Daily News* and the *Dayton Herald* as being open to everyone. Among the women on the reception committee for its Memorial Day and June openings were Sadie Lefkowitz, Dorothy Patterson and Katharine Wright.

Two years later, Patterson gave the club to the city of Dayton outright with a new name: Community Country Club. It was the first municipal country club/golf course in the nation. On the committee for the general dedication in 1918 was Rabbi David Lefkowitz. The Community Country Club placed an advertisement in the May 31, 1918 issue of Dayton's short-lived Jewish newspaper, *Dayton Jewish Life*: "You are now a member of the Community Country Club. This gift to the city of Dayton from John. H. Patterson is to be a recreational spot for all people of Dayton, without cost…membership fees are abolished and everyone in Dayton is therefore a member of the Community Country Club." The High Holy Days 1918 issue of *Dayton Jewish Life* included a half-page advertisement from NCR promoting its cash registers. Advertisements for the Community Country Club in the *Dayton Daily News* at that time also declared, "The park is designed for everyone in the city of Dayton."

Patterson seemed to mean it. Jewish community organizations of all kinds held events and outings at the Community Country Club. Among the groups that held dances there were the Young Men's De Hirsch (Zionist) Club and the Dayton Branch of the Jewish Welfare Board. The Catholic Federation held socials there, the Ancient Order of Hibernians celebrated Irish Day at the club, and the Clergymen's Club—comprising "all pastors of Hebrew, Catholic and Protestant churches" and with Lefkowitz on the Clergymen's Club committee—met there as well. The Salvation Army held its "annual outing for the poor children and mothers of the city" at the club; Jewish-owned Traxler's department store closed for business and held its annual employee outing there; and Jewish-owned Metropolitan Store held promotional picnics there for boys who were members of its Metropolitan Jr. Club.

On May 29, 1921, the Community Country Club dedicated its Oak Tree Memorial Grove "in honor of the Montgomery County men who died in the world war" and presented the grove to the city of Dayton. Leading the presentation to the city was Joseph T. Cline, Patterson's eye doctor. Cline unveiled the stone with the honor roll of names. "The main patriotic address will be given by Rabbi Samuel Mayerberg," the *Dayton Daily News* reported of the rabbi who took over at B'nai Yeshurun in 1920 after Lefkowitz's departure.

Documentation confirms that Black people were also able to use the club, although reluctantly on the part of the Dayton Department of Public Welfare, which oversaw the club for the city of Dayton. An item in the July 26, 1918 issue of the *Dayton Forum*, the local Black American weekly newspaper, related that Dr. L.H. Cox and the St. Margaret's Men's Club "were to be commended" for securing Hills and Dales park for an outing on August 9. "Although this park was given by John H. Patterson to all the people of Dayton, a committee of colored men was recently refused use of the same," the *Forum* article continued. "Dr. Cox went to the 'Powers that Be,' where it was admitted that the park is for all the people, and colored people can secure permission to use the buildings whenever a date is open. Thus, we should contend for our rights and not be continually pushed aside." An article in the September 4, 1919 edition of the *Dayton Daily News* mentions a "colored dance" at the Community Country Club. But it's not known if African Americans were segregated to certain times and locations at the club. A *Dayton Daily News* classified advertisement from July 10, 1918, lists the club as seeking a "competent cook, White woman."

Successful local Jews, who were restricted from the Dayton area's three private country clubs, still established their own, Meadowbrook Country Club on Salem Pike, in 1924. The club opened the following year. Its first president was Egry Register president Milton Stern, and the club's leadership comprised the next generation of mainly German Jews who had established the Standard Club in 1883. Meadowbrook was its successor.

In 1919, Patterson established the East Oakwood Club, now the Oakwood Community Center. He opened it as a nonprofit to serve as an affordable social club for nearby Oakwood residents. There were dances on Saturdays for teenagers and dinners on Tuesdays for adults. According to an oral history, the dinners were prepared and served by "a donated domestic servant, Georgia, and her husband, John."

An item in the May 12, 1921 edition of the *Dayton Daily News* indicates the Council of Jewish Women Annual Meeting and Luncheon was held at the East Oakwood Club, with honored guests Gertrude and Rabbi Samuel Mayerberg of B'nai Yeshurun and Sadie and Rabbi David Lefkowitz returning for a visit from Dallas.

Patterson the Anglophile

There's no evidence to suggest John H. Patterson was personal friends with anyone in Dayton's Jewish community. But there's ample evidence that he built relationships of respect and trust with such leaders as Rabbi David Lefkowitz and Joseph T. Cline. The two were affiliated with Dayton's Reform Jewish congregation, the Jewish religious movement that prioritized comporting with decorum as assimilated Americans. Even so, I suspect something more was at play in Patterson's connections with these two.

In his book *Grand Eccentrics*, Mark Bernstein describes Patterson as an Anglophile:

> *Patterson reached the wholly satisfying conclusion that England's glory, like his own, was a consequence of moral grandeur. Patterson wrote that England "has been for centuries, and still remains, the great civilizer of the world. I believe that her prestige rests on the good that she is doing to the world, and I believe that our strength lies in the good we are doing in the world."*

Cline's parents were born in England. Though Cline was born in Wales, he was raised in Birmingham, England, until he left for America when he was about twenty. Although Sadie Braham Lefkowitz was born in Ohio, her parents, Helen and Louis Braham, were born in England, as were their parents on both sides.

These were not Eastern European Jews whose families had stopped over in England before continuing to America; they were acclimated to English life and culture, as was at least one generation of their families before them.

John H. Patterson. *Courtesy of the Dayton Metro Library.*

AFTER PATTERSON

Oakwood remained steadfastly closed to diversity well past the Fair Housing Act of 1968, which came twenty years after the U.S. Supreme Court had outlawed restrictive covenants (*Shelley v. Kraemer*). Oakwood began opening up to the Jewish community in the late 1970s.

According to the U.S. Census in 2010, 0.9 percent of Oakwood residents were Black, 0.2 percent were Native, 1.4 percent were Asian, 0.6 percent were from other races and 1.6 percent were from two or more races. Only 1.8 percent of the population was of Hispanic or Latino descent.

NCR would go on to hire its first-known Jewish executives in the late 1940s and early 1950s. One was engineer Marshall Mazer, who was hired in 1951 and became a department manager, invented carbonless copy forms and went on to found his own printing and textbook publishing company in Dayton in 1964. Another was Fred Scheuer, who had escaped Nazi Europe for Palestine. Fluent in German, French, English, Hebrew and Arabic, Scheuer worked in the mid-1940s for Mittwoch & Sons, NCR's dealer in Palestine.

Scheuer came to the United States in 1952 with plans to study engineering at the University of California, Berkeley. But when he arrived in New York, he first visited NCR's International Office at Rockefeller Center for a tour. NCR staffers then arranged for him to visit Dayton. Over a meal at Moraine Country Club, NCR's international vice president offered

Scheuer a job with NCR's international education division. "Point blank, straight to the face, I said, 'Isn't it an unwritten law not to hire Jews and Blacks at NCR?'" Scheuer recalled in 2018. The NCR vice president told Scheuer, "It's about time we change that." Scheuer accepted, becoming only the second Jewish executive with NCR at that time (the other was from France and translated instruction manuals). Scheuer established NCR's Latin American technical school in Puerto Rico in 1953–54. In 1955, he transferred to Dayton with his bride, Ruth. Scheuer worked for NCR for forty-three years. He died in 2019.

NCR executives helped the first-known Jewish business in Oakwood succeed, though some neighbors expressed their resistance.

Furrier David Hochstein learned his trade as a teenager. He escaped Nazi Germany at fifteen in 1938 as part of the Kindertransport rescue effort that brought ten thousand Jewish children to live with families in England. An only child, Hochstein never saw his parents again; they perished in the Holocaust. Relatives in London secured him a six-year apprenticeship with the London Fur Company on Regent Street.

After two years in New York following the war, Hochstein opened his own fur business in 1950 in Downtown Dayton. "He had a shop in the arcade," his wife, Clara, recalled. "His *mazel* [luck], next door was the office of the League of Women Voters. He got acquainted with them. One said, 'Why don't you open up a store in Oakwood?'" Clara Hochstein said they drove around Oakwood and saw a "For Lease" sign in an office above 2705 Far Hills Avenue. That's where they moved their business in 1962, but they kept their home in Dayton View.

"We no sooner moved [the business] in there when we got the first letter, sent through the mail," she recalled. "It said, 'Go back to where you came from.'" They received two more letters. "All had the same line, 'Go back where you came from.' David said, 'I'm not going to go back. We're here, we're going to stay here.' I knew we weren't welcome there."

Hochstein Furs remained a fixture on Far Hills Avenue until David Hochstein retired and closed the business in 1988. He died in 2018.

"After a while, I guess they saw that we were nice people, and David did a good job, and they trusted him, and we became very good friends," Clara Hochstein said. Their customers included presidents of NCR and General Motors. "You know, we didn't make a whole *tzimmes* [fuss] about it. David did his job, they appreciated what he did. I worked the front, he worked in the back at his bench. An executive from NCR, I forget his name now, he sent a letter of recommendation with his daughter, and people that came

A 1962 advertisement in the *Dayton Daily News* that announced furrier David Hochstein had moved his business to Oakwood. *Courtesy of Cox Enterprises Inc.*

from all over the world, they sent them to us to buy their fur coats. We didn't have to advertise. It was all word of mouth."

When David Hochstein retired in 1988, he received a letter from the Oakwood City Council: "Your ongoing support of our community has been legendary….As you make plans, remember that you are always welcome in this community."

Postscript: Dayton's First Jewish Cemetery

Beginning with John H. Patterson in 1890 and continuing with his company for over seventy-seven years, B'nai Yeshurun entered into protracted real estate transactions with NCR that would benefit both. At the center of these transactions was the Dayton Jewish community's first cemetery.

The story is almost as old as Dayton's Jewish community itself. It was in 1850 when a dozen Jews organized the Hebrew Society, Dayton's first Jewish organization. The society would become Holy Congregation B'nai Yeshurun, now Temple Israel. In July 1851, Joseph Lebensburger, a leader of the Hebrew Society, purchased an acre "more or less" of farmland from J.W. and Susannah Dietrich outside of the city limits—near the southeast corner of Rubicon and Stewart Streets—to serve as the community's first Jewish cemetery. "It seemed, at the time, that the city's boundaries would never extend so far south," the *Dayton Daily News* wrote in 1915 of Lebensburger's 1851 cemetery purchase. By the 1880s, "the number of Jewish families in Dayton had greatly increased, and it was seen that the burial ground would soon grow unequal to the purpose designed for it."

B'nai Yeshurun's original cemetery near Rubicon and Stewart Streets, with an NCR factory building in the background. *Courtesy of Temple Israel.*

It helped that John H. Patterson wanted the patch of land, around which his factory had grown. In 1890, when NCR had only been in operation for six years, B'nai Yeshurun sold its old cemetery to Patterson and his brother, Frank Patterson, for $3,000. To sweeten the deal, the Pattersons also purchased the congregation's building—which B'nai Yeshurun had occupied since 1863, at the northeast corner of Fourth and Jefferson Streets—for $28,000. B'nai Yeshurun had also outgrown that building, which dated to 1840.

John H. Patterson purchased B'nai Yeshurun's original building in 1890 for use as an NCR salesroom and training center. *Courtesy of the Dayton Metro Library.*

The Pattersons' purchase of the building and cemetery land made it possible not only for B'nai Yeshurun to purchase 6.25 acres in Van Buren Township for its new cemetery, Riverview Cemetery, which it had bought from Anthony and Delia Brown in 1889, but it also allowed the congregation to build its new temple building in 1892 on the east side of Jefferson Street, between First and Second Streets.

Patterson then used the old B'nai Yeshurun building for training and as a salesroom until it was razed in 1911. A *Dayton Daily News* columnist recalled after the building was torn down that the old synagogue was turned into an NCR "agent's school, and then into a building devoted to the advancement of the interests of the members of the NCR household.... The old synagogue building was as wonderful a building as Independence Hall and should have been preserved as the place of the inception and birth of welfare work, which, in its way, is doing as much for the wage-earners of the country as was recorded in Independence Hall on that eventful day years ago."

The June 1934 *NCR Factory News* indicated that with the transfer of the old cemetery property to Patterson and his brother, Patterson still gave B'nai Yeshurun "perpetual rights in the cemetery." Once Riverview Cemetery opened on Cincinnati Pike (now West Schantz Avenue), B'nai Yeshurun's burials ceased at the old site. Some families disinterred and reinterred their departed relatives from among the ninety who had been buried at the old cemetery. Others chose not to disturb the remains. In some cases, B'nai Yeshurun wasn't able to find living relatives to make such decisions.

The story picks up in 1953, when NCR gave Temple Israel 1.82 acres of land from its Sugar Camp complex, immediately adjacent to Riverview Cemetery's eastern border. This was Temple Israel's impetus to reinter the remaining remains from the old to the new cemetery. In 1961, "the grueling tasks of contacting last-known relatives for permission to transfer and reinter the remains began," according to a Temple Israel document from the time.

Although NCR had already purchased the old cemetery land in 1890, it paid Temple Israel $40,000 in 1967 to cover the land, cost of reinterment and improvements to Riverview Cemetery. The disinterments and reinterments took place over four days in May 1967. Workers found and transferred the remains of sixty-two people to Riverview Cemetery. The temple dedicated

The Founders' Circle of Temple Israel's Riverview Cemetery, where the plots that were reinterred from the old cemetery in 1967 are located. *Courtesy of Marshall Weiss.*

this section as the Founders' Circle. Max Kohnop chaired Temple Israel's cemetery committee and directed the transfer operation.

Only the 1.82 easternmost acres of Riverview Cemetery, which the congregation received from NCR in 1953, are in Oakwood. The rest is in Kettering.

Today, the site of Dayton's first Jewish cemetery is paved underneath the parking lot north of the University of Dayton's Raymond L. Fitz Hall, formerly one of NCR's buildings.

9

HOW THE 1917 BATTLE OF JERUSALEM SURRENDER FLAG ENDED UP IN GREENVILLE, OHIO

Few at Israel's December 2017 commemoration marking the centennial of the Ottoman surrender of Jerusalem to the British during World War I would know that the main portion of the surrender flag is housed at a museum in Greenville, Ohio. And visitors to the Garst Museum and Darke County Historical Society in this small city just forty miles northwest of Dayton are more likely aware of the museum's exhibits about Darke County's Annie Oakley and the 1795 Treaty of Greenville with Native tribes, which opened much of Ohio to United States settlement. But for more than fifty years, the 1917 Jerusalem surrender flag has been on exhibit as part of the permanent collection at the Garst. A smaller portion of the surrender flag is on exhibit at the Churchill War Rooms of the Imperial War Museums (IWM) in London. "This flag represents probably the most significant and historic artifact in this museum for what it represents to world history," said Clay Johnson, the president and CEO of the Garst Museum since 2010, and the museum's only full-time employee.

The surrender flag is part of the third major exhibit area at the Garst, which focuses on the life of Darke County native Lowell Thomas (1892–1981), the longtime news correspondent, Fox *Movietone* newsreel narrator and world traveler. Before his radio career with CBS and NBC, which spanned from 1930 until his retirement in 1976, Thomas created the travelogue genre of film. At the urging of President Woodrow Wilson's

Jerusalem mayor Hussein al-Husayni (*center, with cane*) attempts to deliver the Turkish letter of surrender to two British sergeants, December 9, 1917. *Lewis Larsson, public domain.*

Cabinet, Thomas and his cameraman, Harry Chase, embedded with British general Edmund Allenby's army on its way to Palestine in 1917 and captured footage of the campaign.

After the war, Thomas was met with much success when he toured England in 1919 with his two popular travelogues, *With Allenby in Palestine* and *Lawrence in Arabia*; Thomas had befriended British colonel T.E. Lawrence after the Battle of Jerusalem and popularized his exploits. Thomas presented these films with an elaborate stage show that featured lectures and "exotic" music and dancing. According to Royal Albert Hall in London, England, *With Allenby in Palestine* and *Lawrence in Arabia* played there from October to December 1919. "Over 10,000 people a day came to see it, including Queen Mary, who personally congratulated Mr. Thomas in the Royal Box on his eloquent description and his wonderful pictorial record of the campaign."

It was in London in 1919 that Thomas said he received half of the Jerusalem flag of surrender from a Canadian colonel who was responsible for compiling artifacts for Britain's Imperial War Museum. "He came to me one day almost with tears in his eyes," Thomas recalled of the colonel in a 1972 interview with the *Los Angeles Times*. "He said, 'They're piling the stuff out at Crystal Palace, on the outskirts of London, just piling it in heaps, and it's a mess. I think that you, because of your special interest in the Palestine campaign and what you're doing, are entitled to have some of these things, so I've brought you some.'" Thomas added, "He gave me the white flag of surrender—half of it. The other half he said he was keeping."

The flag portion, which measures thirty-five by thirty-seven inches, was part of a cache of artifacts that Thomas donated to the Garst Museum in 1966 for its then-new Lowell Thomas Wing. A page of stationery from the "Department of the Municipality of Honored Jerusalem" that is attached to the portion of the flag in Greenville states: "White flag indicating the Surrender of Jerusalem which was exhibited at junction of Jaffa & Neby Samuel Roads on the morning of December 9th, 1917."

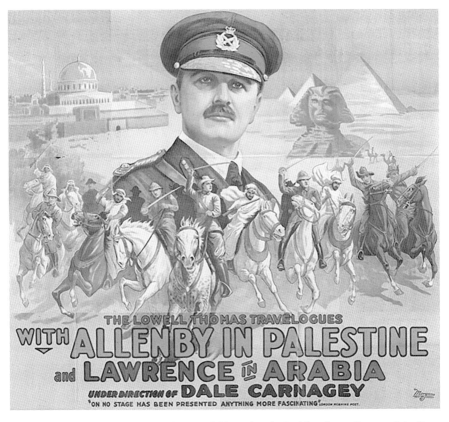

Opposite: Lowell Thomas, a Darke County, Ohio native, in Arabian dress. *Courtesy of the Garst Museum and Darke County Historical Society.*

Above: A poster promoting Lowell Thomas travelogues *With Allenby in Palestine* and *Lawrence in Arabia*. *Courtesy of the James A. Cannavino Library, Archives and Special Collections, Marist College.*

The Garst Museum loaned its portion of the surrender flag to the Imperial War Museums in London for its Lawrence of Arabia exhibition in 2005–6. "The Imperial War Museums renovated and restored the flag as part of the agreement," Johnson said.

In preparation for the centennial of the surrender, curators for a new exhibit at the Tower of David Museum in Jerusalem, *A General and A Gentleman—Allenby at the Gates of Jerusalem*, asked to borrow the flag from the Garst in 2017. The Tower of David Museum is steps away from where Allenby walked into Jerusalem as a "pilgrim" at the Jaffa Gate on December 11, 1917; the victorious general then addressed Jerusalem's citizens from the steps of the entrance to the Tower of David Citadel,

Above: General Edmund Allenby enters Jerusalem, December 11, 1917. *Courtesy of the Tower of David Museum.*

Opposite: A portion of the December 9, 1917 Jerusalem surrender flag, which is on permanent display at the Garst Museum in Greenville, Ohio. *Courtesy of Marshall Weiss.*

with the promise that he would protect all of the holy sites "of the three religions."

Exactly one hundred years later, the Tower of David Museum reenacted the events and officially opened its new Allenby exhibit—without the Garst's artifact. Garst Museum president and CEO Johnson declined the Tower of David Museum's request. "It's sealed away in our case," he said. "We wouldn't be able to loan it." Instead, Johnson provided the curators in Jerusalem with high-definition images of the flag for their exhibit. He also sent them a digital file of a documentary film Thomas produced in 1968, featuring a firsthand account from Thomas's friend Bertha Spafford Vester, the hospital nurse in Jerusalem who provided the city's mayor with the surrender flag.

Overnight on December 8 and 9, 1917, the Ottoman Turks evacuated Jerusalem and handed its mayor, Hussein al-Husayni, a letter of surrender to give the British, ending four hundred years of Ottoman rule over Jerusalem. Before venturing out to surrender to the British on the morning of December 9—also the first day of Chanukah—the mayor visited the American colony. He asked Vester's mother about the proper protocol for surrender. She told him to bring a white flag. Vester took a sheet from a hospital bed, tore it in two, and gave the mayor half to use as the white flag, held aloft on a broomstick.

Lowell Thomas (*right*) with T.E. Lawrence (*left*). *Courtesy of the James A. Cannavino Library, Archives and Special Collections, Marist College.*

That would be the easiest part of the mayor's day. According to several accounts, al-Husayni attempted to surrender six times on December 9; the first four attempts involved low-ranking British soldiers who felt unworthy of the honor or were just confused; the fifth and sixth were with Brigadier General C.F. Watson at 9:30 a.m. and then with Major General John Shea on behalf of Allenby at 11:00 a.m.

It was Watson who, in 1919, had donated the Jerusalem surrender flag to the Imperial War Museums in London. Both halves carry the signature in Arabic of Mayor al-Husayni, who died only a few weeks after the surrender.

Curators with the Tower of David Museum also asked to borrow the Imperial War Museums' portion of the flag—which measures thirty-four by twenty-three and a half inches—"but as we required it for our own displays, the request was rejected," a spokesperson for the Imperial War Museums said.

As of the summer of 2017, staffers at the Tower of David Museum were concerned they would have no surrender flag for their December exhibit, Caroline Shapiro, a spokesperson for the Jerusalem museum, said. "How can you have an exhibit about the surrender without the surrender flag?" Shapiro said. "Then, as staff went through pieces of our collection, one

The Garst Museum, Greenville, Ohio. *Courtesy of Marshall Weiss.*

opened a framed picture, and an envelope fell out of the back with a piece of the flag inside and documentation from the IWM," Shapiro said. "We couldn't believe it."

Along the way, someone had cut and saved a piece of the flag of about twelve by eight inches. According to the Tower of David Museum's records, the remnant was a gift from the estate of the widow of Lieutenant Colonel A.E. Norton, "who collected the flag from the field after the surrender." This third flag portion was part of the Allenby exhibit at the Tower of David, which ran through September 2018.

Johnson said few visitors come to his Greenville museum specifically to see the flag.

> *I have had people come for Lowell Thomas, some researchers, a couple of World War I historians. What this represents is kind of lost here in the United States. The flag, in my opinion, really represents this transformation into the modern-day Middle East. They're* [the British] *the ones that redrew the modern Middle East borders, haphazardly in today's context. It could be argued that they didn't take any of the cultural significance of where the borders were drawn.*

Faced with a generational challenge to keep the legacy of Lowell Thomas relevant—and on a shoestring non-profit budget—Johnson said he aims to "tell the story of history through Lowell Thomas instead of trying just to tell the story of Lowell Thomas."

10
JEWS AND DAYTON'S BOOZE TRADE

It's not commonly remembered today that for centuries, Jews were involved in all aspects of the liquor business in Poland: production, exporting, wholesale and retail distribution and even running saloons. Polish nobility did their best to keep Jews from achieving success individually and collectively—unless the Jews could provide them with help they could obtain from no other source. A census of Jews in 1764–65 recorded that approximately 80 percent of Jews living in Polish villages and about 14 percent of Jews living in Polish towns and cities were involved in the production and sale of beer and vodka, according to the YIVO Institute For Jewish Research. Poland's Jews were able to export Polish grain crops to markets through their connections with Jews in other countries. Jews were also active in Hungary's wine business beginning in the 1700s and in France's after Napoleon opened the ghettos of Central Europe.

So, it's no surprise that when Jews began arriving in America, some joined the liquor trade—and they thrived. The Freiberg family of Cincinnati and the Bernheim family of Louisville became significant donors to general and Jewish causes.

In Dayton, Jews and the liquor trade—and philanthropy—have shared a notable history.

Our story begins in 1859 with Isaac Pollack and Solomon Rauh. Both in their twenties, Rauh and Pollack came to the United States as part of the wave of Jewish immigrants from Central Europe: Rauh arrived

Left: Partners Isaac Pollack (*left*, 1836–1908) and Sol Rauh (*right*, 1835–1915), Dayton's first wholesale liquor distributors, were noted for their Jewish and general philanthropy. *Courtesy of Cox Enterprises Inc.*

Below: An early Rauh and Pollack advertisement in the *Daily Empire*, 1859. *Courtesy of the Dayton Metro Library.*

in 1847 from Essingen, Bavaria, and Pollack in 1850 from Riedseltz, France. They began selling wholesale wines, liquors, brandies and cigars at Third and Kenton Streets. They advertised their business in the *Daily Empire* beginning in September 1859. This was Dayton's first wholesale liquor store.

In 1876, Isaac Pollack and Sol Rauh built identical mansions on lots at 319 and 321 West Third Street in Dayton. *Courtesy of the Dayton Metro Library.*

In 1862, Pollack was appointed a corporal among the Squirrel Hunters, the civilians who assisted the federal government in defending Cincinnati from Confederate attacks.

Partners Rauh and Pollack prospered rapidly. In 1876, they built identical mansions for their families on adjacent lots: 319 and 321 West Third Street in Dayton. According to lore, in the shade of a nearby tree, Pollack and Rauh flipped a coin to determine who would occupy which house; the Rauhs took 321 and the Pollacks took 319. The Pollack House still stands today, though in a different location; in 1979, it was moved to 208 West Monument Avenue and now houses the Dayton International Peace Museum.

Rauh married Jeanette Lebensburger, whose father, Joseph, was the first leader of Dayton's early Jewish community. It was Joseph Lebensburger who, in 1850, established what would become B'nai Yeshurun. Pollack's daughter Hattie married Rauh's nephew Leopold in 1885; Leopold would become the owner of the Egry Register Company and would serve as president of the Dayton Chamber of Commerce from 1908 to 1911.

Rauh and Pollack were among the Jews who lived downtown and worshiped at the predominantly German Jewish B'nai Yeshurun, now Temple Israel. They were founding members of the Standard

Club, the social and literary club that was effectively an extension of B'nai Yeshurun.

A staunch supporter of the Democratic Party, Pollack was a major donor and champion of St. Elizabeth's Hospital when it was established. He was also a member of St. John's Lodge of Masons and Dayton's B'nai B'rith lodge. "His cheerful and amiable disposition won him many friends," the *Dayton Daily News* wrote of him.

Rauh was a director of the Merchants' National Bank and a longtime president of both B'nai Yeshurun and B'nai B'rith. The *Dayton Daily News* described him as "genial, whole-souled and charitable...one of the leaders of this community, and one of the acting spirits in movements that meant the advancement of Dayton."

After about thirty-four years in business together, Pollack decided to split from Rauh around 1893. This was the year when Sol Rauh & Sons, then at 107 East Third Street, began to list itself as also in the distilling business. Pollack retired from his business in 1906 and died two years later at the age of seventy-one. Rauh & Sons kept distilling its own whiskey until

The Sol Rauh & Sons Company building was destroyed in the fire after the Great Flood of 1913. It was rebuilt at the same site. *Courtesy of the Dayton Metro Library.*

at least 1913. The Rauh business was completely destroyed in the fire that occurred immediately after the Great Flood of 1913. Two months later, it advertised in the *Dayton Daily News* that it had relocated and was "now prepared to fill all orders promptly." It continued to list itself as "distillers and wholesale liquor dealers." Rauh & Sons would rebuild and return to its location at 107 East Third Street.

After Sol Rauh's death in 1915 at the age of seventy-nine, his son Ed took over the business. Sol Rauh had brought his sons, Ed and Harry, into the business after he bought out Isaac Pollack. Harry died of pneumonia in 1911. Ed Rauh was a sportsman, well known as an enthusiastic harness horseman. He owned several trotting horses. In 1919, Ed Rauh's business in *Williams' Dayton City Directory* was listed at 107 East Third Street as selling "wholesale non-intoxicating beverages."

An enthusiastically "dry" state, Ohio entered Prohibition on May 27, 1919, nearly eight months before the Eighteenth Amendment to the U.S. Constitution—known as the Volstead Act—went into effect on January 17, 1920. The Volstead Act prohibited the "manufacture, sale or transportation of intoxicating liquors for beverage purposes" in the United States.

Whether or not Ed Rauh went into the soft drink business as a front and remained in the whiskey business as a bootlegger is unclear. Descendants of Rauh who were contacted for this story didn't know the answer. In any case, Rauh's business in the 1921 city directory was listed at the same location but as Rauh's Tire & Auto Supply.

Prohibition's Sacramental Wine Loopholes— and Scandals

To avoid violating the freedom of religion clause of the U.S. Constitution's First Amendment, the federal government did allow exemptions to Prohibition, since Catholics, Jews and some Protestants use wine for religious purposes. Wine could still be produced and sold for use in religious services, and households were allowed to make up to two hundred gallons of wine per year for "non-intoxicating" family consumption.

It was fairly common in those days for Jews to make their own wine at home, and an accepted practice among Jews was to make wine from raisins when fresh grapes were unavailable. A few weeks before Prohibition began in Ohio, Henry Focke's Stores, located in Dayton's Eastern European Jewish neighborhood along Wayne Avenue, advertised in the *Dayton Daily News* a sale on Muscat raisins in bulk, "suitable for wine making."

In February 1920, the federal government set the limit on the sale of kosher wine at a maximum of ten gallons for each individual of the Jewish faith per year for religious use.

The way Jews were to legally obtain sacramental kosher wine for home use under the National Prohibition Act opened up a new set of problems. Congregational rabbis were to determine the quantity to be used by each individual member up to the legal maximum. The wholesale purchase and delivery of wine was either to be made to the rabbi, or the rabbi would provide congregants with the proper paperwork to make a "withdrawal" from an authorized sacramental wine dealer. The congregation was responsible for paying the dealer for the wine based on the rabbi's determination of the needs of his congregants. However, rather than pay the rabbi or the congregation directly for the wine, congregants were directed by the act to make a contribution to the synagogue "for general purposes and not as a payment for a certain quantity of wine."

Add to this that according to Jewish law, kosher wine must only be handled by Sabbath-observant Jews—from crushing the grapes through bottling (unless the wine is boiled)—these policies, which the Bureau of Internal Revenue put in place to safeguard against bootlegging in the Jewish community, would have the opposite effect.

Unlike sacramental wine in Christian traditions, which is consumed in church, wine in Jewish rituals is predominantly consumed in the home; it is used to sanctify the beginning and mark the end of Shabbat each week, for seasonal Jewish festivals and holidays, for circumcision ceremonies and for weddings. Leaders of the Reform and Conservative Jewish movements in the United States saw the potential for abuse of the sacramental wine loopholes. In short order, they urged their members not to use wine for rituals even though it was legal. They encouraged their congregants to use grape juice instead.

The consensus of U.S. Orthodox rabbis at the time was that although grape juice was acceptable, kosher wine was preferable for religious use. Orthodox rabbis, who did not fall neatly into national umbrella organizations as Reform and Conservative rabbis did, saw no reason to refrain from the use of kosher wine, particularly since the U.S. government allowed its use for sacramental purposes.

If Jewish Daytonians didn't produce their own wine, congregants of Beth Abraham and Beth Jacob Orthodox synagogues could procure it through their rabbis via authorized kosher wine dealers in Cincinnati. Board minutes from Beth Abraham Synagogue in 1931 and 1932 indicate the existence of a synagogue wine committee and that Rabbi Samuel Burick gave the board updates on how much wine was needed for the congregation.

Hirsch Manischewitz, a member of the family who owned the maztah-baking business in Cincinnati, was listed in the *American Israelite* as selling kosher wines for Passover in April 1921 at 1410 Central Avenue in Cincinnati (Manischewitz wine didn't appear until 1947). And Rabbi Rudolph A. Funk of Hamedrash HaGadol Synagogue in Cincinnati legally distributed sacramental wine from his store at 1514 Central Avenue in Cincinnati from 1923 to 1925.

According to Marni Davis in her seminal 2012 book *Jews and Booze: Becoming American in the Age of Prohibition*:

> *"Rabbis" (some of whom were not, in fact, Jewish) claimed new and enormous congregations filled with members named Houlihan and Maguire....Rabbis requested wine on behalf of fictitious or long-dead congregants, or sold their legitimately acquired wine permits to bootleggers. The sacramental dispensation also made available a far wider variety of alcoholic beverages than is traditionally present in Jewish practice.*

Leaders of the Reform and Conservative movements, who were more acculturated to American life, recognized that these scandals in the name of religion further fanned the flames of hate against the Jews. Their concerns were justified. Antisemites such as Henry Ford and the newly revived KKK used these scandals of the early 1920s to further pillory the Jews as a threat to American morality.

Davis emphasizes that Americans of all backgrounds were involved in illicit liquor commerce during Prohibition. But the "prevalence of Jewish and Italian involvement" and the attention it received in the press didn't help when the U.S. Congress overwhelmingly passed the Emergency Quota Act of 1921 and the Immigration Quota Act of 1924, which slashed the annual number of émigrés from Southern and Eastern Europe allowed into the United States by 87 percent.

Orthodox rabbis in America at the time—who had been reared in viciously antisemitic Eastern Europe—tended to believe that those who hated Jews would continue to hate Jews no matter what Jews did or didn't do. In a 1991 article for the *American Jewish Archives Journal*, "Orthodox Rabbis React

In step with the Reform movement, B'nai Yeshurun's rabbi Samuel S. Mayerberg railed against Prohibition's sacramental wine exemption for Jews. *Courtesy of the Jacob Rader Marcus Center of the American Jewish Archives.*

to Prohibition," Hannah Sprecher noted that "while rabbis in Europe had essentially ruled over their communities, in America, a rabbi 'at best, found employment with a congregation that gave him little security and meager wages.'" Sprecher summed up that, unlike rabbis in the more affluent Reform movement, "Orthodox rabbis in America were suffering under crushing poverty, and the wine trade was vital to their survival."

One rabbi who publicly railed against Jews' use of sacramental wine was Rabbi Samuel S. Mayerberg of Dayton's Reform congregation, B'nai Yeshurun. This was also the congregation of the Rauh family. As the editorial contributor to the Columbus-based *Ohio Jewish Chronicle*, Mayerberg wrote in the March 2, 1922 issue:

> *In many large cities pseudo-rabbis have been caught with large amounts of wine in their possession. They have been found to be ordinary boot-leggers. When such cases are brought to the attention of the public, they immediately bring the Jewish name into disrepute.*
>
> *While it seems now that it will be impossible to have this harmful law repealed, at least for some time, it is to be hoped that all Jews, be they Reformed, Orthodox, or Conservative Jews, will refrain from the purchase of wines for even religious purposes. Nothing can work greater harm upon the Jewish name than the feeling, which is prevalent, that all Jewish rabbis are boot-leggers and that every Jew does his best to circumvent the national Prohibition law.*

Mayerberg wrote to a colleague in 1926 that he believed in temperance, not Prohibition:

> *I personally believe that the enactment of the Prohibition laws has brought more harm than good. I know that we have more drunkenness in Dayton today than we ever had before Prohibition and I know that our workhouse is filled with violators of the Prohibition laws. It has not reduced crime and has not ameliorated conditions of poverty.*

In 1925, when sacramental wine withdrawals were at their peak, the federal government reduced the amount of sacramental wine available to families by half. It also took away the two-hundred-gallon-per-home winemaking permit, revoked all existing rabbinic wine permits, required that all rabbis reapply and continued to tighten restrictions and bookkeeping safeguards.

The lowest point in the sacramental wine scandals of the 1920s hit in 1926, when a federal grand jury investigated six hundred rabbis in New York City for greatly exaggerating the number of people in their congregations. A family in Dayton's Jewish community got caught up in the federal government's 1927 liquor raids. "Swooping down on the city, apparently without any notice, 20 federal prohibition officers and two state dry raiders, visited a series of residences in various parts of the city, late Saturday afternoon and Saturday night, arresting 21 persons on charges of possession and sale of liquor," the *Dayton Daily News* reported on Sunday, July 3, 1927. Among those arrested, the *Daily News* reported, were Max Solomon, forty-nine; and his wife, Sarah, forty, of 627 Wayne Avenue.

Max Solomon was born in Romania. His first wife, Leah Cohen, appears to have died before Max and his children arrived in Dayton in 1910 by way of England and Canada. Sarah Levison, who was born in the Russian Empire, married Max in Dayton in 1918, at which time Max was listed as a cabinetmaker with the Dayton Wright Airplane Company in Moraine. Dayton's 1927 city directory listed him as a machinist.

"Arrests were made on evidence previously submitted to [U.S.] Commissioner Hudson and on purchases alleged to have been made at the places where the raids and arrests were followed," the *Daily News* front-page story continued. The *Daily News* reported on July 6 that the Solomons were released on a writ of habeas corpus on July 5. The federal judge "had attacked the methods of the raiders, in releasing the two prisoners." But by July 9, the *Dayton Herald* reported that the Solomons had been arrested again that morning. The *Herald* reported "the action marks the reopening of the federal rum war in Dayton."

Two months later, Max's son Sam Solomon, twenty-two, was arraigned in Dayton Municipal Court on a charge of perjury for giving false evidence in a liquor hearing, the *Herald* reported on September 10, 1927. The city prosecutor ordered Sam Solomon, "who was released on a $1,000 bond on a transportation of liquor charge Friday, to be brought into court and compelled to furnish further bail." The *Herald* reported that Sam Solomon had claimed that three men had robbed him of fifty-five dollars the week before. In grand jury testimony on charges of robbery, the three men said they took five gallons of liquor from him "because he had cheated them in a previous whiskey deal. He denied that he had had any liquor dealings with the men."

On November 12, 1927, the *Herald* reported that Sam's father, Max, had been indicted by a federal grand jury for a violation of the liquor act.

Rauh Switches to Near Beer

How did Ed Rauh fare as the decade progressed? In 1924, he was listed in the *Williams' Dayton City Directory* as the manager of the Miami Valley Brewing Company. He oversaw the legal brewing of near beer at Dayton's only remaining brewery plant. In August 1923, the *Dayton Daily News* had announced the project: "Many new formulas have been obtained through which Rauh and his associates hope to make the new near beer so palatable that Daytonians will show a decided preference for it, Rauh says." Whether or not his venture was also a front for full-strength beer is lost to history.

According to Curt Dalton in *Breweries of Dayton: A Toast to Brewers from the Gem City, 1810–1961*, the Miami Valley Brewing Company was the successor to numerous breweries that operated at First and Beckel Streets in Dayton beginning in 1865. Among the owners of breweries at that site were George Weedle and Nick Thomas.

In 1906, several Dayton breweries, including Nick Thomas, merged into the Dayton Breweries Company to fight the growing strength of the Prohibition movement, which was already strong in Ohio. When Prohibition was on the immediate horizon, the combined company continued to lose business. One by one, the seven breweries that made up Dayton Breweries Company closed as the state went dry, until the First and Beckel site was the only one left.

An advertisement from the *Dayton Daily News*, August 14, 1923. *Courtesy of Cox Enterprises Inc.*

In April 1933, with the death of Prohibition in sight, the Miami Valley Brewing Company announced it had been sold to a syndicate of businessmen, including Rauh in Dayton and brothers I. George Kohn and Morton Kohn of Cleveland. With Rauh as manager, they invested $100,000 into the plant to expand and modernize bottled beer production. The brewery was also the first in Dayton to produce beer in cans. But Ohio's liquor commission had concerns about the Cleveland investors and only issued the Miami Valley Brewing Company a temporary permit on June 23, 1933.

Leonard S. Becker was with the Miami Valley Brewing Company from 1934—after Ed Rauh broke off from the company—until 1949, the year before it closed. *Courtesy of the Jewish Federation of Greater Dayton.*

The *Dayton Herald* reported the next day that the brewing company's bond holders "were granted a temporary permit until August 1, by which time, a reorganization is to be effected whereby certain Cleveland interests which recently planned to take over the brewery are to be eliminated." The article added that the permit was granted on the condition that the Miller-Becker Company, Leonard Becker and the Gold Bond Beverage Company and their stockholders, partners, wives or relatives have no "interest, control or management directly or indirectly in the local company or any corporation formed to take over the brewery under penalty of forfeiture of the permit granted." The *Herald* added, "for some time past, that state and federal authorities were investigating the Cleveland interests which had recently taken over the brewery because they were not satisfied with the past records of the new owners."

The Kohns had also brought part-owner Leonard S. Becker from Cleveland to serve as treasurer and sales manager of the Miami Valley Brewing Company.

A month later, the *Herald* was able to report that the state liquor commission had granted the Miami Valley Brewing Company an indefinite extension on its permit and agreed to allow Becker to continue his association with the company. Dayton attorney John Froug, who represented Becker at the hearing, told the commission that Becker had no business connection with the Miller-Becker Company of Cleveland—which Becker's father owned—and that Becker was in business for himself at the Dayton company. The Kohns also stayed on with Miami Valley Brewing.

By November 1933, Rauh severed his connection with the brewing firm; he died five years later at the age of seventy-three.

Becker would become an active member of Dayton's Jewish community. He was elected president of the Zionist Organization of America Dayton District in 1942 and became president of the Jewish Community Council of Dayton (now the Jewish Federation) in 1949, a crucial time of emergency campaigns to bring displaced persons out of Europe and to help the fledgling state of Israel. He left the brewing company around 1949 to oversee Ralph Kopelove's scrap metal business in Dayton. Becker died at the age of eighty-two in 1989.

I. George Kohn departed the Miami Valley Brewing Company in 1946. The plant closed in 1950, after Morton Kohn's death.

A Double-Killing Near Prohibition's End

Dayton police detective Sergeant Tom Wollenhaupt and Detective H.A. Reed arrived at 3219 Princeton Drive in Dayton View on Friday afternoon, June 16, 1933, to find Meyer Ostrov standing in the front yard of the house with a German Luger automatic pistol in his hand. They also saw two men dragging someone by his legs across the front porch. Wollenhaupt then noticed another man lying in the rear seat of a car parked on the driveway. The man in the car told the detective he had been shot and asked to be taken to a hospital.

Inside the house, the living room had been shot up. Ten bullet holes riddled the walls, floor, ceiling, a window and window screen and a chair. A pool of blood soaked the carpet. In the basement, a massive still was in operation, and large vats contained thousands of pounds of mash to produce bootleg liquor. The *Dayton Daily News* described the still as "one of the largest ever taken in the county."

The house was where Lola and Alonzo Dorman lived. At the time of the killings, she, her father and her stepson were in the house. All of the bullets found in the Dorman living room had been fired from the two pistols taken from Ostrov at the scene. The man sprawled on the front porch, Glen "Fat" McCrosson, thirty-five, of Dayton, was dead. He had hemorrhaged to death when a bullet severed his left subclavian artery. Slumped in the car was Lonnie Carmer, twenty-eight, of Newport, Kentucky. He took five bullets: one in the right arm, one in the chest, two in the abdomen and one in the leg. Carmer would die the next day at Good Samaritan Hospital. Both men were known racketeers. Both had been shot with bullets from Ostrov's two guns. Ostrov, thirty-seven, was charged with second-degree murder in the slaying of both.

Meyer Ostrov. *Courtesy of the Dayton Daily News Collection, Special Collections and Archives, Wright State University.*

Born Meyer Ostrovsky in Newport, Kentucky, to Jewish immigrants from the Russian Empire, Ostrov arrived in Dayton from Cincinnati in 1928 to open a local branch of the Western Malt Company of Cincinnati, first at 230 South Main Street in Dayton, then at 521 East First Street. By 1932, the Ostrovs lived at 3775 Ridge Avenue. Ostrov's operation supplied local retail dealers with malt products such as malt syrup. He distributed near beer as well. Ostrov also entered the jewelry auction business as a partner with promoter and auctioneer Jack Werst.

But Dayton's city commission passed two ordinances in October 1930 that, according to the *Dayton Daily News*, "put an end to all jewelry sales except those of established houses here that are passing out of business" because of "the difficulty experienced in making adjustments where jewelry purchased at auction is unsatisfactory because not as represented or for other reasons."

At a Dayton City Commission meeting on March 29, 1932, attorney I.L. Jacobson proposed a new ordinance on Werst's behalf to again permit and license jewelry auction sales; Werst and Ostrov had recently purchased a large stock of jewelry. Ostrov and Emmett Jackson of Dayton's Better Business Bureau began arguing at the meeting, the *Herald* reported, and "Ostrov grabbed Jackson by the tie and commenced to throttle him, but bystanders intervened." The city commission voted on April 6 three to two to retain the ordinance against jewelry auctions. Werst complained that jewelry merchants opposed his operations because of his ability "to sell standard jewelry at a figure below that charged by regular Dayton merchants."

It was Werst who drove Ostrov to the Dorman home on the day McCrosson and Carmer were fatally shot. Along for the ride in Ostrov's car were employees of Ostrov: Henry Hornsby, a son-in-law of Lola Dorman; Thomas Johnson; and Delbert Giehl. Johnson and Lola Dorman's stepson, Robert Dorman, would drag McCrosson's body out of the Dorman house and onto the porch. In Ostrov's car, police found a loaded sawed-off shotgun and three revolvers.

A day after Ostrov was arrested for murder, the *Herald* noted that "police say that Ostrov does not have a record but that they know him as a 'big shot' in the liquor racket but have never been able to get anything on him. They believe that he has a number of stills in operation and that Mrs. Dorman was one of his employees."

A month before the killings, Ostrov was under federal surveillance. On May 10, 1933, "he came near to being the cause of a gun battle between two federal officers and policemen," the *Herald* reported on June 22, 1933. Two federal officers followed a truckload of sugar from the Western Malt Company; they were sure it was headed for a still. But the driver knew he was being followed and returned to Western Malt. Another employee of Ostrov, John Tankersley, got into his own car and followed the truck as it left the store again. When he saw the federal officers following the truck, Tankersley drove up to the side of their car. One of the federal agents—thinking Tankersley was going to push them off the road—drew his revolver and laid it on the steering wheel for Tankersley to see. Tankersley gestured to the truck driver to return to the store. When they did, Tankersley told Ostrov what happened.

According to the *Herald*, "Ostrov, breathless with excitement, rushed to [police] headquarters and reported there were two men, armed, 'laying on his place.'" Four police cars with seven officers converged near Ostrov's store, where the two federal officers were sitting in their car. "With guns drawn, the officers approached the two federal men, who immediately produced their credentials."

Longtime Dayton trial lawyer David C. Greer, who has written extensively about the history of Dayton's legal community, said there was a high level of gangster-related violent crime in southwest Ohio in the 1920s and 1930s. "Hamilton, Ohio, was often referred to as little Chicago since it was essentially owned by the mob," he said. "Midway between Dayton and Cincinnati, it kept both cities busy."

The *Dayton Daily News* reported on June 21, 1933, that "numerous complaints of liquor and gambling rackets being conducted almost openly and without hindrance for the past several months have been received." Local law enforcement was convinced the McCrossan and Carmer killings marked the culmination of a gang war.

In his 2020 book *The Dean, Dillinger, and Dayton, Ohio: Legend-Lore-Legacy*, Dayton Police historian Stephen Grismer wrote that the double shooting was "as much about emerging local gang warfare over rival revenue interests as it was about booze."

> *In this case, gambling and racketeering shakedowns were in the mix. This war may have begun when two henchmen of reputed local gangster and major 35-race-horse "books" operator, Floyd Shawhan, bludgeoned a rival nearly to death. It ended the following year when one of Shawhan's local henchman, Glen "Fats" McCrosson, and another gangster, Lonnie Carmer, were killed by Meyer Ostrov....Protecting criminal interests was brutal and often fatal business, locally as well as nationwide.*

The *Dayton Daily News* reported the day after the McCrosson and Carmer killings that local law enforcement authorities believed they were somehow connected to a hijacking incident a week before.

> *Carmer, the authorities said, sent a truck load of whiskey either to or through Dayton. It was seized by McCrossan, it is said. Two days ago, Carmer came to Dayton to square away with the gangs here and held a long conversation at the Princeton address. While there, he became acquainted with the fact that there was a huge still and as much as 4,000 gallons of whiskey in the making, in the house. This, the authorities said, was used as a wedge to strengthen his demand for money for his allegedly stolen whiskey. If payment was refused, he intended to notify police about the still. That is one angle the officers are probing. Another is that Carmer brought four members of his own gang from Newport, Kentucky here, made McCrossan a virtual prisoner and was using him to extort money from Lola Dorman, who occupied the Princeton Avenue home. Still another angle, authorities said, is that a man who occupies a house near the Dorman home was at sword's points with both the Dormans and McCrossan and tipped the Newport gangsters off to the hijacking episode.*

Ostrov's attorney, A.H. Scharrer, entered a plea of not guilty at his client's arraignment. Ostrov's grand jury criminal trial began on November 22, 1933, in common pleas judge William W. White's courtroom.

Details and photographs were splashed across the front pages of the *Daily News* and *Herald* for the trial's duration, just as the double-shooting had been five months earlier. The courtroom was packed daily with spectators, including McCrosson's and Carmer's widows and Ostrov's wife.

On the second day of the trial, Ostrov admitted through his attorney that he had fired the shots that killed both men, but Ostrov said he had done so in self-defense during a scuffle. At issue in the trial was who owned the still and who fired the first shots. The prosecutor, Calvin Crawford, told the jury he would connect Ostrov to the operation of the large still at the Dorman house, that Ostrov came out to the Dorman house that day to protect his property. Ostrov's attorney, Scharrer, said he would prove Ostrov wasn't connected to the still, that he came to Lola Dorman's aid because she was the victim of a shakedown from McCrossan and Carmer and that they might have been the men who had attempted to shake down Ostrov earlier and even threatened to kidnap one of his children.

Deputy Sheriff Harry Kinderdine testified on November 24, 1933, that he heard Ostrov say in the presence of Deputy Sheriff Lou Janning, "I shot both men—I emptied both guns."

Ostrov had already been acquitted of a murder charge in Cincinnati in 1915. He was tried for the killing of John Collins in a fight during a "drinking party" at a hotel, according to police records.

The McCrossan/Carmer case was riddled with puzzling twists. On the day that culminated with the double-killings, Lola Dorman had contacted Ostrov to help her deal with McCrossan and Carmer; she said they told her they were federal agents and had harassed her and her family for hours on and off at her home since the previous day. Ostrov had his partner, Werst, call Detective Sergeant Tom Wollenhaupt, with whom Werst had a rapport. Wollenhaupt and Detective H.A. Reed drove to Ostrov's business, and Ostrov asked them to head to the Dorman home to investigate the situation. But by the time the detectives had arrived at the Dorman house, Ostrov was already there—he had already killed McCrossan and Carmer.

Wollenhaupt testified at the trial that neither he nor Reed had any idea that Ostrov intended to go out there after Ostrov had asked them to go out and investigate, and Wollenhaupt said that Reed, who was driving, misunderstood the directions to 3219 Princeton Drive, taking Riverside Drive there instead of Riverview Avenue, which delayed their arrival at the scene. Wollenhaupt also testified that Ostrov had told him he went to the Dorman home because "he had never seen McCrossen and he wanted to go out and see what he looked like." Wollenhaupt added that Ostrov told him that as soon as he got out of his car, Ostrov ran to the house and saw a large man standing in the doorway. Ostrov said he thought it was Wollenhaupt. "He told me that as soon as he got in the house, 'they' started shooting," Wollenhaupt testified.

Ostrov had told Coroner Maurice Cooper during an inquest into the killings that when Ostrov arrived at the Dorman home, he thought the police were already there.

> *A big man motioned for me to come in, and I thought that it was the police, but when I got into the house, I discovered it was McCrosson. He grabbed me as soon as I got into the house. I did not know what was happening. Then I saw Carmer coming towards me with a gun. He started shooting me, and I twisted around behind McCrosson and pulled my gun out. As I pulled my gun out, McCrosson started grabbing for it, and while we were struggling for the gun, it was discharged. I don't know whose finger pulled the trigger. I had both guns at different times during the shooting, which only lasted a few seconds.*

Ostrov also told the coroner that he and the men who had come with him were attempting to get McCrosson and Carmer to the hospital when the police arrived. During the trial, Deputy Sheriff Lou Janning testified that Ostrov had told him that McCrosson and Carmer were removed from the home because Ostrov "believed the men might need air."

And then, a bombshell: Prosecutor Calvin Crawford revealed he had a death-bed statement from Carmer that was taken at Good Samaritan Hospital a few hours after the shooting. But Judge William W. White refused to permit the admission of Carmer's dying declaration to the jury, which, by then, had been published in the press. The *Herald* reported on November 28, 1933, that White "stated that the supreme court has ruled that in order to be admissible, a dying declaration must be made not only when the dying person making it is in a dying condition, but that such person has abandoned all hope and expectation of recovery at the time of such declaration." Although toward the end of his death-bed statement, Carmer said yes when asked "Do you realize that you are about to meet your maker?" at the beginning of the statement, Carmer was asked "Do you think you'll pull through, Lonnie?," to which Carmer replied, "I hope so, anyway, pal." That bar wasn't high enough for the judge.

In Carmer's statement, he said he knew the Dorman home was a bootleg place, that he and McCrossen had come there to shake down Lola Dorman for whiskey, not money, that neither he nor McCrossen was armed and that three men came into the house, said, "Stick 'em up," and started shooting with two pistols apiece.

On the witness stand, "star witness" Lola Dorman testified that Carmer fired the first shot. When asked by Prosecutor Crawford whether she got the whiskey still from Ostrov, she said no. But when he asked her who provided her with the still, Dorman refused to answer on the grounds that it would incriminate her.

The jury of seven women and five men deliberated for almost eight hours on Saturday, December 2, 1933. On their sixth ballot, they reached the verdict that Ostrov was not guilty. "As soon as the court was adjourned, many of the women spectators who had attended the trial daily broke into tears and wept profusely," the *Dayton Daily News* reported on December 3, 1933. "Men friends of the defendant formed in a line to congratulate Ostrov and his attorneys."

Nearly a year later, on December 1, 1934, attorney I.L. Jacobson settled a $25,000 wrongful death lawsuit against Ostrov that McCrossen's widow had filed. The *Daily News* reported that the settlement was made after Ostrov paid her approximately $1,000.

With an eye on the end of Prohibition, Ostrov expanded Western Malt Company in 1933 to become Western Distributing Company, a regular-strength beer and wine distributor. In 1938, Ostrov's wife, Gail, was listed as the president of the company, and their son, Harold, was listed as the general manager. Stephen H. Mendell, who was vice president of the Keilson Cigar Company in Dayton, came over to Western Distributing in 1944 as its secretary-treasurer and then as its president.

By July 1948, when the *Dayton Herald* reported that Western Distributing Company had received illegal credit terms for its purchases of beer and wine, the operation was already in receivership. A state liquor department hearing in June 1948 showed that Western Distributing Company had been receiving credit of up to sixty days for its purchases of beer and wine. "Ohio law provides that no wholesale or retail liquor handler may buy malt or brewed drinks or wine except for cash," the *Herald* reported. As a result of Western Distributing's illegal acceptance of credit, the state liquor department banned twelve firms from distributing their beer and wine in Ohio, pending an investigation into their credit practices.

Claims against Western Distributing exceeded $80,000. Attorney James C. Baggott was named Western Distributing's receiver on May 22, 1948. He shut down its sales a month later to liquidate the business.

That same year, Mendell went to work for Mogen David Wine Corporation as its sales manager for Ohio and West Virginia. His sales for Mogen David were so high that he was named its control states manager, coordinating sales functions with Mogen David's individual state managers. Mendell continued working for Mogen David through the 1970s.

Ostrov died in Miami in 1955 at the age of sixty.

11

VICTORY DAY

Jews From the Former Soviet Union Recall the Nazi Surrender

On May 9, 2010, there were fewer guests in the activities room at Covenant Manor in Trotwood than in previous years. Each May 9, there were fewer guests. Those who were able showed up to celebrate Victory Day.

Most of the world marks the defeat of Nazi Germany on May 8. However, those with ties to the former Soviet Union celebrate May 9 as the end of the war; that was when Moscow officially learned the Germans had surrendered.

Covenant Manor is a fifty-unit apartment complex that was developed under the U.S. Department of Housing and Urban Development. The Jewish Federation owned Covenant Manor from its opening in 1983 until 2016. Eighteen Covenant Manor apartments were home to Jews from the former Soviet Union on this 2010 Victory Day.

The Jewish Federation had settled nearly 200 Jews in Dayton from the former Soviet Union between 1989 and 1993 through United Jewish Appeal's Passage to Freedom and Operation Exodus campaigns. These campaigns brought 150,000 Jews from the former Soviet Union to the United States and nearly 1 million to Israel. The oldest among them were either made to fight in the Soviet army during World War II or survived the horrors of the Holocaust—only to languish for decades amid antisemitism and persecution in the Soviet Union.

For these fourteen guests in 2010, the trip to the party was a short one—an elevator ride down from their apartments. Almost everyone brought a homemade Eastern European delicacy to proudly share. "This

The annual Victory Day celebration at Covenant Manor, May 9, 2010. *Courtesy of Marshall Weiss.*

day was the day when all Jewish people received salvation," said eighty-eight-year-old Mandel Shapochnik, who displayed his Soviet army medals on his suit jacket. He was a chemical instructor with a Soviet artillery unit and fought from 1941 to 1945, including at the Battle of Stalingrad and the liberation of Alexandria, Greece. "I was born in Romania," he said. "And this part of Romania, in 1940, was occupied by the Soviet Union. So, when World War II broke out, I was a Soviet citizen."

The first Victory Day, in 1945, also marked the occasion when Shapochnik met his wife, Fanya. "When we celebrated this Victory Day on the central place in our town, we met, and two months later, we got married. I came from the military hospital, and she came from school in Moscow. She had been in a concentration camp." He and Fanya were married for sixty-four years before her passing in August 2009.

Though Shapochnik didn't recall experiencing antisemitism in the army, he said it was part of everyday life after the war. "Stalin was a very bad person," he said. "He planned to destroy all the Jewish people after the war."

Donyel Polotsky, eighty-three, was in Berlin on the first Victory Day. Born in Belarus, he served in the Soviet Army from 1942 until 1954. He still had his medals from the Soviet army but didn't wear them on Victory

Soviet army World War II veteran Mandel Shapochnik shows pictures of himself and his wife, Fanya. They met on the first Victory Day. *Courtesy of Marshall Weiss.*

Day or any other day. "It's not my country," Polotsky said. "These medals are from the Soviet Union, not from America."

Benada Naydorf, eighty-three, was born in Ukraine. Her daughter Lyudmilla Naydorf translated for her. "Yes, my mother was in the ghetto, Zhmerinka Ghetto, Ukraine," Lyudmilla Naydorf said. "She was more than three years in the ghetto under the Nazis. A lot of people died in the ghetto. They died because they didn't have any type of food. She worked in the ghetto. She worked on the railroads, very hard work." Lyudmilla Naydorf said her mother was very lucky; Benada Naydorf's mother, father and sister also survived. "She married Grigoriy Naydorf," Lyudmilla Naydorf said of her mother. "In his family, people died."

Moshko Fishman was eleven in 1941, when the Nazis came to his city in Ukraine. "When they came in July, they moved all Jewish people in a concentration camp, Doroshivka," he said. "Around was barbed wire. Most young people died, and old people died. I have two sisters-in-law and two brothers who died in the camp." Fishman and his wife, Rukhlya, came to

Left: As a teenager, Benada Naydorf survived in a Ukrainian ghetto under the Nazis for three years. *Courtesy of Marshall Weiss.*

Right: David Schmerzler holds a portrait of himself as a soldier with the Soviet army in World War II. *Courtesy of Marshall Weiss.*

Dayton in 1992, three years after their son had arrived here. "He talked me into it," Fishman said. "'Father, come to me,' he said."

David Schmerzler, eighty-seven, was born in Poland. "In 1939, Poland was divided, half to Germany, half to Russians," he said. "We came under the Russians." The Nazis raped and killed his sixteen-year-old sister. Schmerzler, too, served in the Soviet army. "This victory, for me, is amazing," he said, "because for me, from the family we had—eighty persons—three are left. Can you imagine?"

Schmerzler said he always hoped for one unified celebration to commemorate the victory over the Nazis. "Victory was done by the Americans and the Russians together," he said. "It was one victory. And the people should reunite, because we have to work with the young generation, which will replace us, to not be like this was. We have to talk to children and teach them to be friends with all of them, but not give any possibility to fascism in the world."

12

BLACK/JEWISH RELATIONS

From the Dayton Riots Through School Desegregation

"It was Bound to Happen" was the headline of Anne M. Hammerman's column on September 8, 1966. The editor and general manager of the *Dayton Jewish Chronicle* wrote that city leadership "was alerted to a possible riot weeks earlier."

In the early morning hours of September 1, 1966, a White man fired a shotgun out of his car window and killed a Black man, Lester Mitchell, on West Fifth Street. The event, which appeared to be a random drive-by shooting, triggered the worst riot in Dayton history.

One thousand national guardsmen were sent to the lower West Side of Dayton, where they remained for five days. "It just tore the city apart," said Daniel L. Baker, who was a police officer stationed on the West Side when the 1966 riot broke out. Baker and his wife, Gwen Nalls, are the authors of the 2014 book *Blood in the Streets: Racism, Riots and Murders in the Heartland of America*, which covers the period from 1966 through the desegregation of Dayton Public Schools in 1975. "The area was burned out," Baker recalled of the vandalism, fires and looting that ensued in the rioting along West Third Street, the retail center of Dayton's predominantly Black West Side. "Many merchants never came back. And many of them were Jewish owners. After 1966, the city was in pretty significant disarray."

Bruce Brenner was seventeen when the first riot hit West Dayton. His parents owned a grocery at West Fifth Street and Western Avenue. "After a couple of days, we went back in there because there was meat and produce we had to go through," Brenner remembered. "Our store did not get

Dayton police officers clear the streets in the aftermath of the West Side rioting, September 1966. *From the collection of Daniel L. Baker and Gwen Nalls.*

any damage. Basically, the general consensus through the residents of the neighborhood was that for the merchants that treated the people fairly, they saw that when troublemakers came into the area, they helped protect those businesses and kept people from damaging them."

Another Jewish business owner with a shop on West Third Street at the time of the 1966 riot concurred. "I had no loss during the insurrection," said the business owner, who requested anonymity. "I had some customers stand in front of my place and said not to touch it. Police asked me to board up the windows." He added that though it took a while for business to get back to normal, he didn't think about leaving.

That some Jewish businesses were vandalized and looted on the West Side knocked the Jewish community off balance. Since the beginnings of the civil rights movement, Jewish communities across the United States—including in Dayton—were publicly vocal supporters of the cause. Jews were among the founders of the Dayton Urban League, including Temple Israel's Rabbi Selwyn Ruslander, and in 1958, Dayton's Jewish Community Relations Council (JCRC) officially endorsed desegregation and fair housing. That same year, Dayton's Jewish Community Council (predecessor to the Jewish Federation) reported in its newsletter that "community members have been receiving 'hate literature' of the most vile form…to convince the reader that Jews are the power behind the movements of Negroes for equal opportunity." Dayton's JCRC, chaired by Dr. Louis Ryterband, coordinated early lobbying for the 1964 Civil Rights Bill.

"I thought there had always been a very healthy, respectful relationship between Jewish people and African Americans," said U.S. District Judge Walter H. Rice, who arrived in Dayton in 1962. "Jewish people were present at the founding of the NAACP, marched with King, and were civil rights activists," he said. "I kept reading and kept being told that a lot of the Jewish people who had run retail establishments—not only in West Dayton but throughout the country—used to exploit their Black customers. The Jewish people were shocked: they had tried so hard to be good landlords, good shopkeepers."

Rice, who was then in private practice in Dayton, recalled a Jewish businessman from the West Side who told him that he had a long list of debtors, people who owed him money, "because he carried those people through bad times, and he was shocked to find out that they felt he was a racist."

Hammerman expressed concern about these negative Jewish stereotypes in the pages of the *Dayton Jewish Chronicle*: "There may have been a few here and there who milked their customers of a higher rate of interest—but by and large, our people have done much to elevate the West Side of Dayton, and they do not deserve these false accusations."

"I think from then on," Rice said, "there has been a feeling of wariness between the two groups. Just like a friendship, you feel that you are simpatico with someone, and then, all of a sudden, find that each of you retains deep suspicions and distrust about the other. So, I think it has changed. Not permanently, not beyond repair. But it put a burden on the relationship."

Blood in the Streets author Daniel L. Baker, whose family migrated to Dayton from Kentucky, grew up on the predominantly White East Side. His wife and coauthor, attorney and realtor Gwen Nalls, grew up on the West Side. Nalls is Black, Baker is White.

The title of their book doesn't just refer to the riots in Dayton of 1966, 1967 and 1968; it follows the murders of serial killer Neal Bradley Long from Dayton's East Side, whose random shootings of Black men on the West Side in the summers of the early 1970s ratcheted up community tensions even higher. In 1975, Long would kill Charles Glatt, the desegregation specialist who was hired by Dayton Public Schools to oversee integration of the district.

Though it was never proven, Baker is convinced it was Long who killed Lester Mitchell in 1966, which sparked the first riot. "I grew up in the middle of all this," Nalls said. "My parents are from Mississippi. They migrated here for work. When they came to town, General Motors was here, every major industry was booming. My mom was a day worker. She went to work for a Jewish family, cleaning their home." Baker observed that the migration pattern of Black and White people coming to Dayton from the South for jobs—with the White population on the East Side and the Black population on the West Side—only solidified the segregationist nature of the city.

Gwen Nalls. *From the collection of Daniel L. Baker and Gwen Nalls.*

Joan and Dr. Charlie Knoll moved to Dayton in 1956 from northern Ohio. They recalled Dayton being solidly segregated. "There was an unwritten law that you did not put African American patients in the same room with non–African American patients," Knoll, a longtime physician said. "And the first hospital to break that [rule] was Miami Valley." He successfully pushed to have St. Elizabeth's integrated.

Joan Knoll worked as a secretary at the VA hospital, where she befriended women who were Black. When she would ask them to join her downtown for lunch, they would always decline. "Finally, I asked, 'Is it because of the difference of our skin?'" she said. "'No, we can't eat lunch at Rike's. We can't go to a movie downtown.' These were professional women. Social workers and so forth. They were upper-class women."

In 1960, Rice and his first wife, a native Daytonian, were planning their wedding in the city:

> *We had some African American friends from Pittsburgh that we wanted to invite. And my prospective father-in-law called several hotels and was told they couldn't stay there. And finally, they were accommodated at the Van Cleve Hotel, only because my father-in-law threatened to move the wedding elsewhere; it was scheduled for the Van Cleve.*

Ellen Faust and her parents came to Dayton in 1936, when she was three months old. Her father opened a store on West Third Street, and the family lived in the back. She and her husband, Howard Faust, a pharmacist from Cincinnati, settled in Dayton in 1959. Armed with her education degree, she interviewed with Dayton Public Schools. She said:

> *Places like Fairview High School were all White, certainly, there were no Black teachers. The assistant superintendent at the time, the head of personnel, interviewed me for the job. And he said, "I need teachers at Roosevelt and at Fairview. You wouldn't want to teach at Roosevelt." Dunbar High School was an all-Black school, and Roosevelt was a mixed school.*

At Fairview, Faust taught chemistry and general science. "At one point, a Black student who came to register—the family had moved into the district—was told, 'You'd be more comfortable going somewhere else.' So, there were very deliberate attempts to make sure that Black students had only some access, and there was nowhere to go to protest that kind of thing."

Faust said she became an activist in civil rights when Sis and Rabbi Selwyn Ruslander's daughter, Gail Levin, was president of the League of Women Voters. The Fausts are congregants at Temple Israel, where Ruslander was then its rabbi. "The League of Women Voters did a study of education and looked at segregation in Dayton schools," she said. "And that was probably the first time that I looked at it seriously."

For Knoll, it was her work with the Council of Jewish Women that brought her to civil rights activism. "The National Council of Jewish Women had a store on West Third and Broadway," Knoll said. "Dorothee Ryterband ran it. They sold secondhand clothing to people with low incomes." She recalled that it was Dorothee Ryterband who saved the store during the 1966 riot, "when she handed out sodas to the soldiers and the rioters in front of the store. Little bitty Dorothee. She was gutsy."

Faust also became involved with the Council of Jewish Women. "The council always had as its basis, social action," she said. "With that, the council was considered the Jewish group for women that you had to belong to to be socially acceptable."

Along with Dorothee Ryterband, Sybil Silverman led the council's charge on racial justice activities.

A year later, on September 16, 1967, in the midst of a Shriner's convention in Downtown Dayton, a police officer shot and killed a Black man he thought was carrying a gun. When it turned out to be a pipe, the policeman planted a gun on the man's body.

Dayton police officers with fixed bayonets in the riot zone on West Third Street, 1966. *Courtesy of the* Dayton Daily News *Collection, Special Collections and Archives, Wright State University.*

Another riot ensued, this time, urged on by activists from out of town, including H. Rap Brown. That's when Ellen Faust and Joan Knoll started marching, their kids in tow. "We marched with the rabbis and Protestant ministers, priests and nuns," Knoll said. One influential member of the Jewish community told Knoll's husband that "if his wife kept on doing these things, he was going to lose his practice," Knoll recalled. "You see, it was hard to talk people into doing what wasn't fashionable. Ellen and I were bad girls."

Rioting continued in 1968, following the assassination of Reverend Martin Luther King Jr.

"It Was Just Out of Control"

Since the early 1900s, the Emoff family had a furniture store on West Third Street. "I remember going to the store pretty frequently with my dad at two in the morning, when he got a call that his windows were broken,

The national guard in Dayton, September 1966. *Courtesy of the* Dayton Daily News *Collection, Special Collections and Archives, Wright State University.*

probably three or four times," said Mike Emoff. "And we'd go down and meet the police there, and the windows would be smashed in the front. I didn't understand it. I didn't know what was happening. I was maybe eight to twelve. Those were the sixties, almost seventies. It was just out of control."

Emoff said his family kept the store there in the years right after the riots.

> *That's where they started. My dad got along really well with the residents of the West Side of Dayton. Even though all that happened, the riots were more of an emotional type of reaction, and it didn't matter whose store was there, there were people who just looted and smashed. I was young, so I didn't get a lot of that, but I looked through the news clips I found when my dad died. Some of that stuff bothered him, obviously. He kept it.*

"I couldn't understand the riots," Nalls said.

> *I couldn't understand why. I remember hearing it on TV, and I'd ask my parents, what sense does it make for them to be burning down our backyard? And to this day, I don't understand it. Even today, you can go and see it never really got back to what it was.*
>
> *Rap Brown and those guys, their focus was, "I'm going to get your attention by burning it down," which is the Ferguson approach: not only are we not going to support your establishment, we're not going to let anybody else in.*

Baker described West Dayton in the summer of 1966 as a tinderbox. "The Civil Rights Act was passed in 1964, and in the United States, it was not well-received in many places," he said. "And then the Watts riot in California happened in 1965, the worst riot in this nation's history." According to the Associated Press, forty-three riots tore across U.S. cities through the summer of 1966, including in Chicago, Cleveland, Atlanta and San Francisco.

Baker recalled that in May 1966, the *Dayton Daily News* presented a series called *West Side '66*; it addressed issues of segregation, poverty in the Black community, lack of education and police brutality. "And guess what? In all of those articles, many of the Black leaders of the time predicted this place is going to blow up if we don't fix some of this," Baker said. "One guy said if it gets above ninety-five degrees here this summer, this city's going to explode."

Judge Rice remembered that police/community tensions in 1966 were raw. "The police, frankly, treated members of the community poorly, with disdain and lack of respect, and were perceived—not in an exaggerated

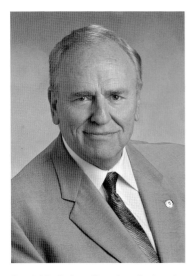

Daniel L. Baker. *From the collection of Daniel L. Baker and Gwen Nalls.*

fashion—as an occupying army," Rice said. "It's sad to say, but in many areas of the community, while the police tactics changed, the tension still exists."

Rice found himself on an extradition case in Los Angeles on the next-to-last day of the Watts riots in 1965, when he was with the Montgomery County Prosecutor's Office. Although he said the Dayton riot of 1966 was not as bad as Watts, it made indelible changes on the city. Fear on all sides was palpable. "Within about five years, the neighborhood was almost a ghost town as far as retail overall," he said.

West Dayton, on the whole, Rice said, was fairly integrated then. "Inner West was African American, but Outer West off Third had a lot of White people. So, not only did you have the flight of the White middle class, you had the flight of the Black middle class as well. And the neighborhood, for about twenty years, was left to die." One of the areas where members of the Black middle class migrated to was Dayton View, then the hub of the Jewish community.

Despite the Supreme Court's 1954 mandate in *Brown v. Board of Education* for public schools to desegregate "with all deliberate speed," Dayton Public Schools all but ignored the order until it faced a 1972 suit that was brought by local families and the Dayton NAACP. As the suit made its way up to the U.S. Supreme Court and back to the U.S. District Court, activists in Dayton's Jewish community would join the fight to desegregate the school system and attempt to keep the atmosphere as peaceful as possible.

The Attempt to Desegregate

Even before Melissa Sweeny began attending high school at Colonel White in 1970, she heard about tensions in the building between White and Black students. "There were what they were calling riots," she recalled. "I can't say that it was full-blown riots. But it was definitely turbulence in the schools, where the kids would be fighting." She remembered her mother, Elaine

Fairview High School's 1974 varsity basketball team. The year before, the squad was all White. *From the collection of Mike Emoff.*

Bettman, telling her to get inside because a crush of high school students was running down the street. "And we were a good mile from school," she said of their home on Harvard Boulevard, across from United Theological Seminary in Dayton View. "When I was in high school, I remember the same kind of thing happening, and I had to escape into a doctor's office on my way home," Sweeny said. "And there was a day when stuff was going on in the high school, and someone lit a girl's afro on fire. And she's running through the halls with her afro on fire."

In the years after the West Dayton riots of 1966, 1967 and 1968—and the destruction and exodus of several businesses along West Third Street—those in the Black community who could afford to move elsewhere did so. One area that wasn't restricted to minorities then was Dayton View, the neighborhood where most of Dayton's Jews lived at that time.

Dayton's organized Jewish community supported integration and the formal process to desegregate Dayton Public Schools. But as the desegregation order was carried out, the quality of public education in the district declined overall. With crime and vandalism at their doorsteps, Jews were not immune to White flight.

"There were an awful lot of disciplinary problems. People weren't used to getting along," said U.S. District Judge Walter H. Rice, whose children attended Dayton Public Schools at the time. "I remember my older child being afraid to go to school," Rice said.

There was an arts program that served as a magnet school. It brought people from all over the community, and my son in fifth and sixth grade was simply afraid to attend—not because of the Black students and not because of the White students, but because there was so much Black/White tension and fights that he simply didn't want any part of.

Mike Emoff lived three houses down from Fairview High School. In 1974, when he was a sophomore, he remembered Dayton started a busing program. Emoff's parents didn't want to disrupt his education. Though his younger brothers would attend the Miami Valley School, a private, nonsectarian prep school in Washington Township, he remained at Fairview, with approximately fifteen Jewish kids in his grade. "It was probably one of the best things that happened to me personally because I learned how to deal with a world that wasn't all perfect," Emoff said. "My parents went to Fairview, my grandparents went to Fairview. It was mostly Jewish at one point. And it's gone today."

At Colonel White, Sweeny said there wasn't busing, since the student body was already integrated, nearly 50–50 by the time she graduated. Four or five of her classmates were Jewish; most Jewish students went to Fairview in Dayton View or to Meadowdale in Northwest Dayton. "The White kids that didn't want to be with the Black kids had their side of the high school," Sweeny said of Colonel White. "They hung out on Wabash. And then you had the Black kids, who were hanging out in front of the high school, and they never mixed."

Sweeny said she was part of a middle group that went either way. "There was actually a group that I started talking to about that—there were probably about twenty-five of us—to go on little mini retreats," she said. "The thought was if those of us that were involved in this could spread it to the rest of the school, then maybe it would calm things down," Sweeny said. "Of course, that didn't work, because there were too many opinions on how this should be going. The White kids that were on the Wabash side were not interested in becoming friends with the Black kids, so that really wasn't going to go anywhere. We really thought we were going to be doing something, but it didn't help anything."

Emoff said he was pretty close with the dozen or so Jewish students in his grade at Fairview. "We had that Jewish connection, so we were in that tribe-ish kind of mode, I suppose," he said.

As Fairview students were bused out and students from other neighborhoods were bused in, they formulated their own tribes as well.

"They had their tribe from Roosevelt, guys that knew each other, and they came in and we were taking their turf," Emoff said. "All the Jewish guys stayed on the sidelines and didn't get in the middle of any race relations stuff. It was kind of an opportunity for me to learn how to deal with a lot of different kinds of people. I was friends with the new kids, I was friends with the old kids, I wasn't intimidating to anybody."

Gwen Nalls, a lawyer and realtor, grew up on Dayton's West Side. She recalled that as a Black girl in Dayton's public school system, her second-class education ill prepared her for higher education. Nalls graduated from Dunbar High School in 1972. "My teachers would talk to us, not necessarily as a class. They would tell me that at Belmont, they have these kinds of labs, they have these kinds of instruments, they have these kinds of resources," Nalls said. "And then you come over here and you get hand-me-downs if you have anything. There was always this dual system. What really manifested itself was when you went to college, when you had to do entrance exams, when you have to try to compete or even keep up, you realized, we never had that. We weren't taught that."

Fairview High School's 1974 varsity tennis team. All but one of the team members were Jewish. *From the collection of Mike Emoff.*

In the late 1960s, Dayton's school board and its superintendent were at odds. Superintendent Wayne Carle was a champion of desegregation. The school board was not. To help keep a watchful eye and peace at the schools experiencing natural integration, Carle recruited a network of mothers to volunteer as teacher's aides. Among them was Joan Knoll, who volunteered through the Council of Jewish Women. "There was an African American group that was analogous to the Jewish women," Knoll said. "A lot of people didn't like us because we were too close to Wayne Carle. Because we were too liberal, and he was too liberal."

Frustrated with Dayton's segregated schools, minority families and the Dayton Chapter of the NAACP filed a federal suit against the district in 1972. U.S. District Judge Carl Rubin initially approved the Dayton plan to bus students voluntarily for limited sessions at environmental science centers. "It wound up being a good move, even though it was not intended to be that," said Dayton city commissioner Jeff Mims of the initial science centers.

Mims has served as a city commissioner since 2014. He began his career in 1970 in Dayton as a teacher's aide through a Model Cities program. "They were looking for minorities who lived in the community and who were veterans to become potential teachers because it was evident at that time that Dayton Public Schools did not have a high number of minority teachers, and the number of minority students was increasing."

In 1973, Mims was hired to teach art in relation to science at an environmental science center at Eastmont Elementary School. "The students got a total of sixteen days per year in that environment," he said.

> *The first year, we had some challenges. We had a group of parents from Ruskin School* [on Dayton's then Appalachian East Side] *that actually came to Eastmont attempting to shake the bus. They got carried away, and slowly, they were about to turn the bus over, and then one parent said, "Oh! The kids are still on the bus." And so, they stopped for that reason.*

When Mims was assigned to teach social studies at Belmont High School, he already knew 80 percent of the students—Black and White—since he had taught them at the science center as elementary school students. "I ended up in a situation where the kids would be fighting or doing some crazy things," Mims said, "and I'd walk up to them and ask them to stop, and they'd look up and say, 'OK, Mr. Mims.' And the principal said to me, 'Who the hell are you?'"

Desegregation specialist Charles Glatt, who was murdered by Neal Bradley Long in 1975. *Courtesy of the Dayton Daily News Collection, Special Collections and Archives, Wright State University.*

The NAACP appealed Dayton's limited magnet approach, and the plan was eventually deemed insufficient. By the summer of 1975, Rubin assigned Ohio State University desegregation expert Charles Glatt to devise and implement a comprehensive desegregation plan for Dayton Public Schools.

Irate at the thought that his children on the White East Side of Dayton would be bused to go to school with Black children, Neal Bradley Long began his killing spree in the summer of 1972, randomly shooting Black people on the West Side in the early hours of the morning. For the next three summers, he would continue to shoot at least thirty Black men, killing seven.

When Glatt was assigned to desegregate Dayton's schools, Long killed him at point-blank range in Glatt's Dayton office. It was Daniel L. Baker, a Dayton police officer at the time, who took Long's confession to the thirty previous shootings. Glatt's murder, Mims said, gave the mission of desegregation more purpose.

Dayton's NAACP needed to raise $60,000 for its legal fees connected to the 1972 federal case. It was Lou Goldman, the president of the Jewish Federation of Greater Dayton, who helped organize the fundraising, recalled Jessie Gooding, now a Dayton NAACP former president who was Dayton NAACP's vice president at the time. "Lou was always friendly to the NAACP," Gooding said. To assist with the federal case, NAACP's national office had a cadre of lawyer volunteers who were Jewish. "The national director of the NAACP at the time, you could call him in the morning, and that evening, with no money, he'd have a lawyer in Dayton," Gooding said. "I can remember three or four Jewish guys he sent down here. He'd send them to Dayton overnight."

Before the federal appeals court insisted that Dayton Public Schools get on the track to real desegregation, members of Dayton's Jewish community were actively involved in trying to get levies passed and desegregation-friendly candidates elected to the school board. One of those candidates who ran in 1973, unsuccessfully, was Ellen Faust. "By then, the school board had a large representation of people who were for segregation and the continuation of it," Faust said. "That side called itself Save Our

Schools (SOS). The business community in town formed a group called CBS, Citizens for Better Schools."

A key desegregation leader in the Jewish community at that time was Carol Pavlofsky. "She was just out there recruiting women," Knoll said. "She had a crew of women reporting to her."

Peter Wells, retired executive vice president of the Jewish Federation of Greater Dayton, arrived in Dayton in 1973 as an assistant to the federation's executive director. "Where we were mostly involved in the desegregation process was as observer members of the Metropolitan Churches United, the interdenominational organization," Wells remembered.

> *The churches took a role in trying to pull the community together: corporate, labor, the religious community, the nonprofit community, the Black community and the police. Church leaders went to the corporate people and said, "You may live in Oakwood, but you work in Dayton. If Dayton burns, you burn." And that led to a peaceable desegregation.*

"I knew what they were feeling," Baker said of the Jewish community. "When the big fights would happen at Colonel White all those years ago, a lot of Jewish families lived right there on all those streets around there," said Baker, who lived in Dayton View at the time. "It was a shame. And they spoke out, wanting and trying to lead peaceful resolutions to those things and put tremendous pressure on the school board and the police department, as they should have, to try to come to some resolution."

"We had rallies and we had meetings," Joe Bettman said. "We once rented a yellow school bus, and they had a parody song of *Yellow Submarine*, and we're all in this yellow bus, going around the neighborhood, trying to rally some support."

Desegregation activists weren't just going after Dayton's schools; they attempted to convince suburban districts to become part of the plan. They knew it was the longest of longshots. Joe Bettman was invited to a Kettering PTA meeting to debate a vice president of the Kettering Board of Education about the pros and cons of desegregation. "The hall was filled," Bettman said. "Well, they really gave me a hard time, and a few shouts here and there."

If there were Jews who didn't support desegregation, they kept it to themselves. "Jewish leaders knew what it was like to be disenfranchised and second-class citizens in the eyes of many," said Robert Weinman, an assistant superintendent of Dayton Public Schools when desegregation took place. "So, how could we, with our backgrounds and our history, stand in the way?"

"A lot of the young people who were from the area where a lot of Jewish families lived, they were more amenable and understanding in accepting the different cultures," Mims said. Even so, there were incidents. But incidents brought the potential for teachable moments.

When one of his Jewish students disrupted his class, Mims told her to move her seat. At first, she refused. "I said, 'move to this location,' and so, as she picked up her books to move, she said, 'Black fucker.' I took my pen out, and I'm saying this out loud to the whole class as I'm writing her up: 'I asked student to move to newly assigned seat. In the process of moving, she called me a Black fucker.' I said to her, 'Here, take this to the office.'" She returned to school after her three-day suspension when Mims's class was creating jewelry. "And so, I sit down with her. I was working with her because she was making this necklace and earring set that she wanted to wear to the prom," Mims said. "And all the kids are looking, because they think I'm going to be mad at her. And so, we got along fine. And after about three days, she apologized. She said, 'I'm really sorry.'"

At Fairview High School, Emoff recalled the trouble that came "from all the White jocks who were there. They were competing for different status levels at the school, like the football team and the basketball team. Some of the White kids that came in came from the North Dayton area, the rough White kids, were the ones who were bumping heads with the Black kids." Emoff said some students were killed in the fights. "Somebody shot himself in my backyard," he said. "It was a White guy who was just depressed because he was stressed with school. There were five suicides, Black and White, in those last two years, not all at school. And there were a lot of drug-related things that were happening at school."

Emoff and other honors students at Fairview were bused three afternoons a week to participate in the district's high school honors program at the YMCA downtown. "Fairview had dropped its honors programs because that wouldn't have achieved the objective within the school," he said.

Another dimension to Emoff's perspective was the kidnapping and murder of his grandfather, furniture store owner Lester C. Emoff, in 1975. "My grandfather was kidnapped by three Black guys, one of whom is still alive and still in prison; the other two have died in prison. And they shot and killed him. That did not sit well with me, obviously. But I didn't let that seep into anything at school. I just kind of stayed to myself."

Along with other members of the middle class, Jews began moving out of Dayton View to Northwest Dayton, the suburbs north of Dayton, and a few to areas south of town, for several reasons. "Kids would start stealing their bikes," Dr. Charlie Knoll said about his children when he and his wife began thinking of moving. "Aaron got a new bike, someone stole it off the front porch. We had a Thunderbird. People came along and threw bricks through the windshield."

Former Dayton Public Schools assistant superintendent Weinman said some families who chose to remain in Dayton boosted enrollment at private schools, such as the Miami Valley School and Hillel Academy Jewish day school. "As I look at my fellow religionists, we're a strange group," Weinman said. "We'll give our money, in fact, sometimes, we'll give even our life to help. But when it comes to our own families, we want the best education for our youngsters. Because of deseg, you're bringing in a less-well-educated group, which can [academically] harm those that are ahead."

Nalls said White flight was a self-fulfilling prophecy. "The schools are going down, and when you pull your kids out, yes, it went down."

Baker said of the Jews of Dayton View:

> *I can relate to what their feelings were, the mixed feelings about being in an area you feel is a progressive area, an accepting area. That's what Dayton Triangle was clearly all about. I have to admit, I was a real sucker for believing all that for a long time, too—the urban pioneer. Until my house was broken into twice, my car stolen three times, and my teenage daughter was abducted at gunpoint by a drug addict at her morning school bus stop in 1984. Thank God she was recovered by police five hours later. I said, that's enough. Get out. So, you say to yourself, "How much social consciousness do you have?" But what you do is protect your family.*

What We Did and Didn't Learn

Thursday, September 2, 1976, marked day one of Dayton Public Schools' implementation of its court-ordered desegregation plan to achieve racial balance. According to an Associated Press story, the first day of busing students across the city went "as smooth as silk," with no demonstrations of any kind. It had also been nearly a year since serial killer Neal Bradley Long had shot and killed Charles Glatt—the Ohio State professor who was assigned by the federal court to carry out the desegregation order in Dayton.

"We won the desegregation, but we didn't win anything," said Jessie Gooding, who served as a vice president of the Dayton NAACP at the time.

Dayton's NAACP chapter was a driving force behind the 1972 federal lawsuit to integrate Dayton Public Schools, a case that would make its way to the U.S. Supreme Court and back to federal district court. Gooding would lead Dayton's NAACP as its president from 1985 until 2003—a year after Dayton NAACP and Dayton Public Schools reached a settlement to end the failed desegregation program. "The schools are more segregated now than they were in the seventies," Gooding said.

Dayton NAACP former president Jessie Gooding. *Courtesy of the Dayton NAACP.*

"It was the law of unintended consequences," said U.S. District Judge Walter H. Rice, who inherited oversight of the implementation of the desegregation order for Dayton Public Schools when he was appointed a federal judge for Southern Ohio in 1980. "The motives were good, but it precipitated not only the flight of the White middle class, but also the flight of the Black middle class," Rice said. "And that's when Dayton's descent into poverty, I believe, began because areas were left with no White or Black middle-class role models or mentors."

From 1960 to 2016, Dayton's population plummeted from 262,332 to 141,527. Student enrollment in Dayton Public Schools went from 60,633 in 1965 to 14,000. "It went like a rock," said Daniel L. Baker. "No matter what else was being fixed inside the city, it was clear that the city was going to decline because of the population. Probably one of the most significant things that drove so much movement out of the city was the fact that they elected to do a district-wide plan, not a regional plan like Indianapolis or other places where Dr. Glatt had been. No one would have had the stomach for a regional plan anyhow."

Joe Bettman. *Courtesy of the Jewish Federation of Greater Dayton.*

Joe Bettman was among the desegregation activists who attempted to persuade suburban districts to join Dayton's desegregation efforts, fully knowing how unlikely those districts would be to sign on. "How can you desegregate if you don't have anybody to desegregate with?" Bettman said.

"A national education maven had set up desegregation in Tampa and one other city, and he came to speak to us in Dayton," Bettman said.

> *His theory was if you integrate the schools and do the busing of the kids from the White neighborhoods and so on—because you have to remember, back in those days, there was very segregated housing—if you did that, the kids from very disadvantaged homes would show improvement in their scholastic achievements, and the kids from more advantaged homes would not suffer their education. That was the theory.*
>
> *Unfortunately, about five years after all this happened, I pick up a* Parade *magazine from the Sunday paper, and this guy disavows: he misinterpreted his statistics. It was really devastating. We had worked so hard.*

Rice pointed out that at the time of Dayton Public Schools' desegregation, housing opened up, "where it was no longer permissible to deny a person housing because of race, color or religion."

When asked what could have been done that might have brought more success to the attempt at desegregation, Rice said:

> *Other than barricading people into specific neighborhoods, I don't know what could have been done. In the last ten to twelve years, there has been a conscious effort on the part of government to disperse housing, to place lower-income or lower-middle-class income Whites and Blacks into suburban communities. Had that occurred sooner, it might have eased some of the problem. But the political will was not there to do that in the 1970s.*

Dayton city commissioner Jeff Mims taught at Belmont High School when desegregation was implemented. He would go on to serve as the president of the Dayton Education Association, president of the Dayton Board of Education and as a representative on the Ohio School Board, the state teacher's union. "The sadness of it is—because society hadn't done what it needed to do then—they forced the schools to do their job in terms of desegregating society," Mims said.

> *The other sad part is they did not give us what we needed. The only thing they gave the schools was a little bit of money for transportation. They did not give schools money for a strong level of professional development and training in helping the teachers and administrators understand why we're doing what we're doing, what we're doing, and the purpose in terms of the whole process. We were left to figure it out on our own.*

Even so, Mims said the attempt at desegregation produced more pluses than minuses. "It gave people a better sense of the fact that we had good people—White and Black—and we had bad people—White and Black," Mims said. "And that neither race has a corner on the market. It gave people a better view of human dynamics. If the teacher was comfortable enough and used those teachable moments, it became a success."

Robert Weinman, an assistant superintendent of Dayton Public Schools at the time of desegregation, said the integration of Black and White teachers brought them together as friends, "not just on school issues, but personally, as they got to know each other better."

Dayton city commissioner Jeff Mims. *Courtesy of Dan Cleary.*

"There were an awful lot of disciplinary problems," Rice recalled.

> *People weren't used to getting along. But the one thing I think we got out of [desegregation] that I don't think should be overlooked is we learned to coexist with each other on an equal basis. I mean, Blacks and Whites had always interacted, but it was almost like an employer/employee basis. But here, our kids were forced to go to school together, and they liked or disliked people because they were mean, they were bullies, not because they were Black or they were White.*

"Thinking back, it was very uplifting because we saw good things happening, too, and made good friends through the years, Black and White, and non-Jewish and Jewish," Elaine Bettman said.

"You're talking to people who came through it and survived it happily," Joan Knoll said of herself and her husband, Dr. Charlie Knoll. "And our children survived it happily. It made the [Dayton View] neighborhood more interesting. And now, we live in a neighborhood [Northwest Dayton] where, believe it or not, not much needed to be done. We were already integrated by choice. It just happened."

With Black students comprising 73 percent of Dayton Public Schools' population in 2002, Rice presided over the settlement between Dayton's NAACP and Dayton Public Schools to formally end desegregation in the schools and return to a neighborhood school program. "There simply weren't enough White children," Rice said. At first, the Dayton NAACP resisted Dayton Public Schools' request that Rice lift the busing order. Rice said of the Dayton NAACP:

> *It had been a monumental accomplishment for them, and there was tremendous frustration that it hadn't succeeded to the extent they had wanted it to, and they thought to remove the coercion of the busing order would make things worse.*
>
> *Their position was not totally unjustified because by the time the busing order was dissolved and we returned to so-called neighborhood schools, a lot of those neighborhood schools no longer existed. They had been torn down, condemned as unfit and the like.*

"It fragmented communities," Mims said of Dayton Public Schools' attempt to desegregate. "There could have been so much more that we should have done if there had been more money. It could have been so much better."

Former Dayton NAACP president Gooding said he still thinks the only way Americans will become equal as a society is to desegregate. But he doesn't know when that will happen.

> *The United States is funny. They ain't ready. They ain't got over slavery with Black folks. Somehow or another, they want to keep us subservient for some reason. They're not ready for us.*
>
> *By more than a stretch of the imagination, Obama got to be president. And a lot of the repercussions come as a result of him being president. The hardness came when a lot of folks thought Blacks went too far making him president of the United States.*

"I've seen it all," Gooding said in the summer of 2016. "I know what discrimination is. That's why I'm so scared now, man. I am frightened of Trump. Trump is dangerous. I'm scared if he loses, I'm scared if he wins. You know why I'm afraid if he loses? These people will follow him to start a race war. There are a lot of people who are mad."

Baker, who began his career with the Dayton Police just before the 1966 riot, said the hopelessness he saw in the Black community back then was as profound fifty years later. "Hate, to me, is as prevalent today as it was before."

For decades, Rice has facilitated initiatives in the Dayton area to bridge racial divides. To him, the greatest obstacle is that people don't feel they can truly improve the human condition. And they don't have the drive to understand each other's perspectives. "At the same time, there's been a decline in the effort of faith-based leaders to have a community ministry, to reach out to other parts of the community," Rice added. "These things were the focus of the civil rights movement. I don't think they exist today." Rice said:

> *The reason I think there's a divide, not just between the Jewish community and the Black community, but between the Black and White community today, is this: many people in the White community feel that they worked hard in the civil rights movement. We won. Everyone is on the same plane legally. Now it's up to them* [African Americans] *to move the ball down the field. They have no patience to listen to or to try to understand that racism today is even more entrenched, certainly harder to identify because it's underground.*
>
> *Too many Jewish people say to African Americans—because I've been present—"We know what it is to be Black in the United States because we've been discriminated against and went through the Holocaust." Well, the Holocaust is the worst thing to ever happen to a racially-identifiable group that I can think of. But the average African American will respond, "We understand, but you don't know what it is to be Black in this country every day, to be stopped driving through Oakwood, to be followed in a retail establishment just because somebody thinks, you're Black, so you're obviously going to shoplift."*

The civil rights issues of today, Rice said, aren't about where you can live, go to school or eat. "It's the state of public education, it's the criminal justice system, it's housing, it's banking, it's social services, a thousand other things," he added. The federal judge said that the biggest failure of his professional career has been his inability to work out a consent decree to increase the number of minorities in the police and fire departments.

"It's not that Black police officers would cut people in the neighborhoods a break, it's just that they understand the context in

U.S. District Judge Walter H. Rice. *Courtesy of Peter Wine, the Jewish Federation of Greater Dayton.*

which some of these things are happening, and could better deal with them, and could educate their colleagues on what it is they're policing in different neighborhoods."

Baker, who was a Fifth District police commander on Salem Avenue in the 1980s—and served as a consultant to Cincinnati after its 2001 race riots—agreed.

> *If you look today at some of the major complaints filed by the Department of Justice, we still don't have the appropriate minority hiring in law enforcement. You're still looking at the same bleak economic conditions for a certain subset of people. You have unresponsive government in the eyes of some people. That's what's so troubling; we're repeating that cycle, except today, under the glare of all the social media and the 24/7 news.*

Rice said Dayton's city charter has been the obstacle toward diversifying its police department.

> *And that it's the rule of one: you must pick the next name on the list for a promotion or appointment.*
>
> *You may have someone who scores 100 on the civil service test who doesn't have the common sense to come in out of the rain. But if you could pick between the top five, you might find someone who scored a 90, yet has street smarts, common sense and the like.*

The political will to amend Dayton's city charter came about after the grotesque murder of George Floyd in Minneapolis on May 25, 2020, by police officer Derek Chauvin, who kept his knee on Floyd's neck for nearly nine minutes. The video footage was seen around the world.

Nearly a month later, the Dayton City Commission established a police reform process involving Dayton Police, the Community Police Council and community members to ensure, as Mayor Nan Whaley said, "that Black Daytonians are front and center in this conversation."

Among the 142 recommendations of the police reform working groups was the elimination of the rule of one from the city charter to allow for police and firefighter recruit appointments to be selected from a larger group of applicants.

With the recommendation of Dayton's charter commission, the Dayton City Commission unanimously approved placing the proposed city charter amendment on the ballot for Dayton's May 4, 2021 special election.

Dayton's Fraternal Order of Police lodge opposed the charter amendment. Its president, Jerome Dix, noted in a letter that because the police department had exhausted every examination list in the last decade, the rule of one didn't get in the way of police force diversity, the *Dayton Daily News* reported. "This means every applicant who passed the required civil service test and pre-employment background check, polygraph test, psychological evaluation and physical has been processed for employment," Dix wrote.

Torey Hollingsworth, senior policy aide to Mayor Whaley, said the police reform working group was aware that all examination lists are exhausted when it made the recommendation.

> *The thought here is that the practice doesn't make very much sense to begin with. They wanted to make sure there was the opportunity specifically to have these assessments that may pick up on different kinds of soft skills—community relationships—as you can get in something like an interview. Right now, there's no interview involved in the police hiring process. The community made really clear that they want police who think of themselves as guardians versus warriors. That's something you can only really assess in talking with someone versus a written test.*

Voters approved the amendment 74.2 percent to 25.8 percent.

Rice said American society needs "Jewish, non-Jewish, Whites and Blacks to get to know each other's history, background, and perceptions. And I guarantee you that if we do, then a lot of these problems can be resolved."

BIBLIOGRAPHY

Baker, Daniel L., and Gwen Nalls. *Blood in the Streets: Racism, Riots and Murders in the Heartland of America.* Cincinnati, OH: Forensics Publications, 2014.
Bernstein, Mark. *Grand Eccentrics—Turning the Century: Dayton and the Inventing of America.* Wilmington, OH: Orange Frazer Press, 2017.
Brodkin, Karen. *How Jews Became White Folks and What that Says about Race in America.* New Brunswick, NJ: Rutgers University Press, 2010.
Dalton, Curt. *Breweries of Dayton: A Toast to the Brewers from the Gem City, 1810–1961.* Scotts Valley, CA: CreateSpace Publishing, 2013.
Davis, Marni. *Jews And Booze: Becoming American in the Age of Prohibition.* New York: New York University Press, 2012.
Glotzer, Paige. *How the Suburbs Were Segregated: Developers and the Business of Exclusionary Housing, 1890–1960.* New York: Columbia University Press, 2020.
Greenberg, Cheryl Lynn. *Troubling the Waters: Black-Jewish Relations in the American Century.* Princeton, NJ: Princeton University Press, 2006.
Okrent, Daniel. *The Guarded Gate: Bigotry, Eugenics, and the Law that Kept Two Generations of Jews, Italians, and Other European Immigrants out of America.* New York: Scribner, 2019.
Peters, Margaret E. *Dayton's African American Heritage.* Virginia Beach, VA: Donning Company, 1995.
Ronald, Bruce W., and Virginia Ronald. *Oakwood: The Far Hills.* Dayton, OH: Reflections Press, 1983.

Bibliography

Rothstein, Richard. *The Color of Law: A Forgotten History of How Our Government Segregated America.* New York: Liveright Publishing Corporation, 2017.

Weiss, Marshall. *Jewish Community of Dayton.* Charleston, SC: Arcadia Publishing, 2018.

ABOUT THE AUTHOR

Marshall Weiss is the editor and publisher of the *Dayton Jewish Observer*, which he established for the Jewish Federation of Greater Dayton in 1996. He is also the author of *Jewish Community of Dayton* (Arcadia Publishing, 2018) and the project director of Miami Valley Jewish Genealogy and History, also through Dayton's Jewish Federation. A past president of the American Jewish Press Association (AJPA), he is a founder of the Jewish Scholastic Press Association and the International Jewish Media Forum. He is the recipient of numerous first-place awards from the Ohio Society of Professional Journalists and AJPA. In 2017, he was awarded the Religion News Association's first-place honor for Excellence in Religion Reporting at Small Newspapers. He received his master's degree in journalism from Temple University and his bachelor's degree in philosophy and English from Albright College.

Visit us at
www.historypress.com